EXTREME ENTREPRENEURS

Steve Jobs
and
Jesus Christ

TRACY EMERICK, Ph.D.

BOOKSIDE Press

BOOKSIDE Press

BookSide Press
877-741-8091
www.booksidepress.com
orders@booksidepress.com

Contents

Introduction   1

Chapter 1: What Is an Entrepreneur?   4
Chapter 2: Characteristics of an Entrepreneur   10
Chapter 3: Innovation and Profit   22
Chapter 4: Types of Entrepreneurs   27
Chapter 5: Extreme Entrepreneurs   34
Chapter 6: People or Things   39
Chapter 7: Soul   46
Chapter 8: Soul Powers   52
Chapter 9: Steve Jobs   58
Chapter 10: Jesus Christ   67
Chapter 11: So What?   74

Bibliography   82
About the Author   83

Dedicated to three people who influenced my writing:

Dawn, my wife
Susan, my sister
Deb, my pastor

Introduction

To set the stage, let me offer a quote from an American author, spiritual writer, and Franciscan-friar based in Albuquerque, New Mexico. His name is Richard Rohr. He said:

"Our unique little bit of heaven is installed by the Manufacturer within the product, at the beginning! We are given a span of years to discover it, to choose it, and to live our own destiny to the full. If we do not, our True Self will never be offered again, in our unique form."

Combining the earthly with the Divine is intentional. We all have a bit of the Divine in us, but we may not be aware of it. As you scan the pages of this book, it is my hope that you will *discover, rediscover, or expand* your Divine influence here on earth as expressed by your soul.

For many years, I researched the many lives of entrepreneurs which led me to one important realization and conclusion: *Entrepreneurs imprint whatever they do based on who they are.* What are these imprints?

These imprints are the expressions of an Entrepreneur's soul. The soul is the driving force in everything that they do. Whatever the soul commands, the actions follow.

The two "extreme entrepreneurs" who shaped the world into what it is today and whose lives I expose through this book, used that driving force of their soul to achieve their goals. I hope that, by the end of this book, you will agree that dependence on our soul is essential for a rewarding life – whether to accomplish a goal or build lasting and fruitful relationships.

A "unique bit of heaven" is installed within us and "installed" within our soul. In order to bring this concept to life, this book uses two well-known individuals – Jesus Christ and Steve Jobs. Steve and Jesus endeavored their entire lives to bring their "true self" to

1

the maximum. To do this, they were driven from within by their souls to be the accomplished people that we know them today.

One goal of this work is to expose you to your inner driver - your soul- that, if you follow, will allow you to make the world more meaningful for you and others. Your soul has a life agenda for you. What you need to do is to uncover it. It has been hidden within you for years or even decades!

If you start to let that inner being guide you – your thoughts and actions - your life will be more satisfying and rewarding. Its rewards will elevate your life to the full.

However, the soul that serves as the compass in our lives may not always lead us to the right path. Remember that your soul's interest is you, and its direction may not always yield positive thoughts and actions. The soul's "self-interest" can move you into deception, deceit, and sensual exploration. This is where you need discernment to suppress what might seem like "a good idea at the time." This is where the Divine influence saves the day, guiding you away from self-interest outward.

There is another dimension of the soul that will also be explored. Soul, as the nonverbal communicator, tuned in to all living things. The soul is analogous to the "force" in the movie series, *Star Wars*. However, instead of just a few having the ability to tap into the force, our souls allow all of us to tap in and we do every moment. The irony is that in *Star Wars,* there were those that talked about the force and those that had it. Living things on earth all have it (soul), but as humans, we don't realize what it can do for us.

Each of the extreme entrepreneurs did introduce profound changes to humankind as the expression of their souls. Steve Jobs put easy-to-use technology in the hands of humans, to be used for life enhancement without any need to know or understand the underlying technology. Jesus Christ changed the paradigm of life from one of fear to one of love; giving each of us the opportunity, whether we want it or not, *to be loved and to love.*

Jesus' teachings were not new. The Jews held forth that thou shalt love the Lord your God with all your heart, soul, mind, and

2

strength. But Jesus made a simple addition, that changed the whole love paradigm, when He added, "… and your neighbor as yourself."

It shifted from a love that goes "from us toward an external God" to a love that must begin "with us loving ourselves and then our neighbors and then God".

May the chapters of this book give you every chance to contemplate, understand, and respond to the Divine messages that come to you through your soul.

Chapter 1

What Is an Entrepreneur?

Before we dive into the lives of the two extreme entrepreneurs whose experiences and legacy we will expound in this book, I find it best to align ourselves with a common understanding of an entrepreneur. So let me ask you: What's the first thing that comes to your mind when you hear the word "entrepreneur"?

Like most people, you probably perceive entrepreneurs as purely business people – someone running a business. We often get a vision of coats and ties, suitcases, business meetings, and money-making ventures – these are the common primary perceptions of entrepreneurship. However, there is more to an entrepreneur than the persona of a businessman and the profit-making processes that most people perceive.

Through this book, and the understanding of the two personalities whose lives we will further dissect, I wish that this will change the way you look at entrepreneurship and in effect, bring you lessons that will become eye-opening and life-changing.

Entrepreneur, Defined

Our first task is to have a deeper understanding of an entrepreneur beyond the usual perception. Merriam-Webster defines the word entrepreneur as *"one who organizes, manages, and assumes the risks of a business or enterprise."* Looking at this clear-cut definition, we realize that an entrepreneur is someone who does

4

not only organize and manage a business (profit-making venture), but also an enterprise.

An enterprise is defined by Merriam-Webster as *"a project or undertaking that is especially difficult, complicated, or risky."* Thus, difficulty, complication, and risks are three elements that define an enterprise in which an entrepreneur should organize, manage and assume risks.

In essence, an entrepreneur is also a person who believes he or she can bring forth something that will be more pleasing to people than that which currently exists.

We all can be entrepreneurs at some level. A lemonade stand, for example, is an entrepreneurial endeavor, often time with results that cannot be duplicated. In my case, a card table by the street, a pitcher of lemonade made from ingredients from the kitchen, and a few glasses; and an enterprise was launched, to great success, I might add. Net income was 100 percent mine. However, when the first pitcher sold out and it was time for a second, my mother taught me my first accounting principle—the *cost of goods.* If I wanted a second pitcher of inventory, I had to pay for the raw materials: sugar and lemonade mix. While my profits went down, the venture was a success, putting some disposable income in my pocket. This first entrepreneurial experience would lead to many more lessons and experiences.

Entrepreneur and a Business Enterprise

According to the Global Enterprise Monitor, Babson College, in 2016, over twenty-five million people started or ran their own businesses. The report says this is about 14 percent of the working-age population or about one entrepreneur per seven working-age adults. The number of entrepreneurs is not as significant as what makes them different, and where do entrepreneurs fit in the grand scheme of life?

One characteristic that makes entrepreneurs different from the other six people is entrepreneurs are willing to assume risk in order to accomplish results. Six people will heed Tarzan's advice, *"Do not let go of the current vine until the next vine is firm in hand."*

The odd one out ignores this sound advice and lets go of the vine, in anticipation of grasping the next vine as this is a much faster way to get from point A to point B. Risk is a secondary consideration for entrepreneurs, I know. Various ventures that cost me many thousands of dollars were entered into with great enthusiasm. Only after admitting failure was the dollar investment a concern. I am thankful that other ventures did work out, such that retirement is quite enjoyable.

Risk, therefore, is an element in entrepreneurship - whether it is for profit-making or any kind of venture toward the achievement of a goal. The entrepreneur assumes all the risks and takes the brunt of the consequences that it causes. When there is a success – big or small – the entrepreneur also takes the credit.

The Entrepreneur in the Organizational Structure

Where entrepreneurs fit in the grand scheme of life is a little more complicated. Often associated with business, entrepreneurs are a key part of a team. It is the entrepreneur who has the "big idea" and explains the vision to the other team members, so they can apply their skills and talents in a coordinated way. The entrepreneur, therefore, holds everyone together for the achievement of the enterprise's goals.

To have a better understanding of an entrepreneur's role, it is important that we know where an entrepreneur fits in an organization or a team.

One management consultant, Dr. Ichak Adizes, developed a model of what is necessary to have a team. His model was developed in the '70s and has been applied to thousands of organizations around the world. I found his model quite useful during my consulting days, and even now, it has provided a solid foundation when putting the people pieces of a situation in place.

Dr. Adizes's model is the acronym, PAEI, which describes the four roles that various people play in an organization. These are as follows:

Producer
Administrator
Entrepreneur
Integrator

In Dr. Adizes's model, while all of these roles are necessary for an organization to be successful, not one person can fill all of these roles. A person can perform one or more roles at the expense of doing their best work in the role they prefer.

Boomer alert! In my days in marketing demography for targeting purposes, it always amazed me that the government-defined small businesses as less than five hundred employees. So the term *small business* did not have much meaning when 99 percent of businesses are under five hundred employees. Couple that with the fact that 81 percent of small businesses have no staff, in fact, nowadays, you arrive at a vast number of businesses that have very few staff.

For ease of discussion, we referred to this vast array of businesses as "mom and pop" businesses. These are normally family businesses with two people running the operations. When doing target marketing in a mom-and-pop business, it is highly important to know who the decision maker is in order to properly message an offer to elicit a response from prospective buyers or customers.

But these two-person businesses weren't always family. However, the roles of the two people were distinct to operate the business harmoniously. One person strives to grow the business, and the other makes sure the bills could be paid. Essentially, one is a dreamer, and the other is a realist.

What follows is an attempt to meld Adizes's model with the mom-and-pop model as a way of explanation. To be clear, the melding has nothing to do with gender and only to do with the responsibility of the role a person performs in the business. I made this a *boomer alert!* because I am in the boomer generation and developed my vernacular under different rules that apply today. No disrespect is intended for anyone who might identify, or not, as either a "mom" or "pop."

The four roles defined are the following:

1. *Producer.* The primary goal of any organization is to produce results. The producer's attention is on getting the job done to produce results. They work hard and get things done. In food service, this would be the cooks and servers. In manufacturing, this would be the workers and supervisors. They are often referred to as "line" workers. In insurance, this would be the actuarial and the salespeople. In the typical "Mom and Pop" business, this would be the pop.

2. *Administrator.* Administrators focus on how tasks are completed. They're interested in the rules that help an organization to function. They concentrate on ensuring that people follow procedures correctly. In all organizations, this is accounting, human resources, quality control, and operations. In the typical "mom and pop" business, this would be the mom.

3. *Entrepreneur.* Entrepreneurs are full of ideas. Their souls call them to form a vision or visions, and they may be gifted at building a shared understanding and helping other people share in the vision. They are often described as "risk-takers" or "visionaries." Oftentimes, these are the people running the business. In mature companies, this function is found in the research and development department or through the acquisition of small companies that are still in the entrepreneurial phase. In the typical "Mom and Pop" business, this would more than likely be the pop.

4. *Integrator.* Integrators excel at bringing people together and maintaining harmony within an organization. Their focus is on performance. Their true value is translating the vision of the entrepreneur through the organization's

team(s). This person can be the president, chief executive officer, or executive vice president. One key integrator responsibility is to keep the entrepreneur from burning down the business with the next big idea. In the typical "Mom and Pop" business, this would be the mom.

In this book, we will examine only the "E" person – the entrepreneur. You might find an additional exploration of Dr. Adizes's model useful as he expands on the PAEI and how each type responds to change through Adize's Institute Worldwide (available on Google).

Chapter 2

Characteristics of an Entrepreneur

Before we study the lives of the two extreme entrepreneurs that this book exposes, I find it imperative to dig deep into the characteristics and personality traits that each entrepreneur should possess in order to achieve his or her goals. These characteristics define an entrepreneur and are the keys to success. The most successful entrepreneurs that we know today have elevated their businesses anchored on these characteristics.

These characteristics are considered building blocks to any entrepreneur and are truly visible in the lives of the two extreme entrepreneurs we will expose. Jesus Christ and Steve Jobs come from completely varying generations and backgrounds but the two have common characteristics too – they were driven, committed, and goal-oriented. They were laser-focused on their individual goals.

Entrepreneurs, in general, have characteristics that set them apart from others. These characteristics became part of them and were reflected in their personalities. They mastered these characteristics day in and out.

It is my hope that these characteristics may help also you in your entrepreneurial endeavors or professional life regardless of what industry you currently tread on.

The 12 Characteristics and Personality Traits

I came across an online definition in an article written by Lestraundra Alfred, *"12 Characteristics and Personality Traits Great Entrepreneurs Share"*, published by HubSpot in February 2021. To round out the characteristics of an entrepreneur, I adopted the article here:

Though hard work is often a factor in success, one's level of output does not always determine success in their field—and entrepreneurship is no exception.

There are many factors that can contribute to the success of an entrepreneur as they launch, operate, and scale their business. These factors can include the timing of their business launch, how competitive their market is, the reliability of their supply chain, the amount of capital they are able to obtain, and the current economic climate.

In addition to these elements, there are a number of traits successful entrepreneurs have in common that contribute to their business success. Let's dive into what they are:

Successful Entrepreneur Personality Traits

- Discipline
- Creativity
- Self-Awareness
- Resourcefulness
- Process-Oriented
- Empathetic
- Communicate
- Self-Motivated
- Confident
- Flexibile
- Risk-Taker
- Resilient

Discipline

"We have looked for the entrepreneurship gene and there is no entrepreneurship gene. There is not. It is disciplined execution that makes people successful entrepreneurs." Author, Disciplined Entrepreneurship

Starting and operating a business is no easy feat. Unlike a traditional job where you often have upper-level management driving business objectives and keeping you accountable, being an entrepreneur requires the ability to hold yourself accountable when you don't have a "boss" to do so.

Those who are able to create and execute plants even without external factors holding them accountable have a competitive edge in business. When an entrepreneur has self-discipline they are able to manage the urge to procrastinate and can take decisive action when needed.

Three-time entrepreneur Bill Aulet recognizes that focus and discipline are critical for startup success, and it›s even the focus of his book, *Disciplined Entrepreneurship*. He goes so far as to say, "It is disciplined execution that makes people successful entrepreneurs." His book outlines a 24-step framework for bringing products to market. The rigorous (but fun) methodology comes from Aulet's experience building startups, raising capital, and creating value from shareholders.

Creativity

"I got the idea of having a bake sale every day while listening to a financial guru on the radio." - Founder and CEO, The Cupcake Collection

Though creativity is often associated with artistic output, it is an important trait for all entrepreneurs to have. Creativity doesn't only apply to visual elements or branding. Entrepreneurs who are able to creatively solve problems and think outside of the box when facing everyday business challenges are able to quickly pivot and implement necessary solutions that lead to business growth.

Inspired by a financial guru and the high cost of sweets in her area, Mignon Francois went from "household manager" to founder and CEO. "I got the idea of having a bake sale everyday while listening to a financial guru on the radio. I was a household manager of 6+1 (aka stay-at-home mom) and I really couldn't afford the luxury of taking my children out for sweets because everything was expensive and we were struggling. Once I started to get my recipes together, I would practice all day."

Originally, she didn't even know how to bake, relying on her daughters and grandmother for help. However, her hard work and ingenuity turned a condemned home into a full-blown bakery and a creative endeavor into a ten-million-dollar business.

Self-Awareness

"I suck at 99 percent of stuff, but I go all out on that 1 percent I'm good at." - Gary Vaynerchuk Entrepreneur, Speaker, Author

Entrepreneurs who have a sense of self-awareness that they are able to apply professionally to achieve business success. When an entrepreneur is self-aware they are able to own up to their strengths and weaknesses related to running their business.

With this awareness, they are able to zero in on the tasks and elements of running the business they can excel and are more willing to delegate the areas they are not as strong in. Another benefit of being self-aware is that it increases one's ability to give, receive, and apply meaningful feedback.

Lifelong entrepreneur and social thought leader Gary Vaynerchuk says that self-awareness is a trait he wishes the business world paid more attention to, more so than hustle or smarts.

"Self-awareness at its finest is accepting your shortcomings and accentuating your strengths," he says. In his blog post on the topic, he says that the moment you decide to do so, "things will change."

Resourcefulness

"It's not about money or connections. It's the willingness to outwork and outlearn everyone." - Mark Cuban Entrepreneur, Investor, Media Personality

Many entrepreneurs are faced with tasks and challenges they have never faced before. The ability to be resourceful is a mindset that helps entrepreneurs reach lofty goals without a clear way to achieve them.

When entrepreneurs are able to work resourcefully, they can effectively problem-solve and grow and scale their businesses without having all of the answers or resources to do so. Being resourceful requires a can-do attitude and willingness to work creatively to effectively manage a business without having the immediate know-how.

Mark Cuban — entrepreneur and investor — says that entrepreneurs must have a "willingness to *outwork* and *outlearn* everyone." While having access to money and resources can make a difference, a key part of being an entrepreneur is cultivating those resources yourself. "There are no shortcuts, you have to work hard and try to put yourself in a position where, if luck strikes, you can see the opportunity and take advantage of it."

Process-Oriented

"The message of the Kaizen strategy is that not a day should go by without some kind of improvement being made somewhere in the company." - Masaaki Imai Management Consultant and Founder of the Kaizen Consulting Group

Having solid processes in place is essential for any successful entrepreneur. In the world of business, a process is a repeatable series of steps that help those working within a business to complete necessary tasks. Processes can apply to various aspects of the business including sales, onboarding new team members, production, and product fulfillment.

When business owners have a process-oriented mindset, they are able to work smarter, not harder. Implementing processes in various areas of the business can prevent waste, allowing business owners to scale and grow their businesses. Additionally, when business owners have repeatable processes in place, they are able to easily train new team members to fulfill important aspects of the business without sacrificing time or quality.

Masaaki Imai, management consultant and founder of the Kaizen Institute Consulting Group, says this about processes and systems: "The message of the Kaizen strategy is that not a day should go by without some kind of improvement being made somewhere in the company."

He is, of course, referring to a principle called <u>Kaizen</u> that champions the guiding philosophy of "continual improvement" often applied in lean business and productivity processes. Kaizen's impact can be found in the snowball effect that incremental changes to process can make, and it has been practiced throughout the world — most notably at Toyota as part of the *Toyota Way Fieldbook* and at Trader Joes as one of the company›s core values.

Empathy

"In this day and age, I think empathy is more important than ever. As we scale our company, what will differentiate us in the future is what has differentiated us in the past: We fundamentally care about our customers and each other." - Dharmesh Shah Co-Founder and CTO, HubSpot

Empathy is an essential trait for entrepreneurs. Whether a business owner manages a large team of employees or works directly with their customers as a high-performing solopreneur, they must be able to connect with others on a genuine level.

Successful entrepreneurs are able to put themselves in others' shoes, considering the perspectives of their employees and customers as they navigate key business decisions. In business, empathy can look like anticipating your customer's needs, empowering your team members to take time off to recharge when they need it, and giving both employees and customers space to voice their opinions and concerns.

Business owners who have the soft skills necessary to connect with others may experience benefits such as increased customer loyalty, more customer referrals, and increased employee productivity.

Dharmesh Shah, co-founder of HubSpot, considers empathy such an important core value that he modified the organization's Culture Code to include it. "Not too long ago, I found a bug in our Culture Code that needed fixing. We use the acronym HEART to describe qualities we value in our coworkers. For years, these qualities were: Humble, Effective, Adaptable, Remarkable, and Transparent. But something wasn't right. HEART did not clearly capture one of the values that I think is fundamental and part of our core at HubSpot. That value is: empathy."

Communication

"Leadership is a way of thinking, a way of acting and, most importantly, a way of communicating." - Simon Sinek, Author, Speaker

According to research from Wroclaw University, the top three communication skills for leaders are effective listening, getting a message across clearly and vividly, and providing feedback in a supportive manner.

These skills can put entrepreneurs at a competitive advantage. When a business owner is able to effectively listen to their customer, they are able to implement customer feedback that can help them improve their offerings. Additionally, when business leaders exhibit these skills with their own employees and team members, they are able to build trust which can improve productivity and business performance.

Communication is a big part of Simon Sinek's message to business leaders. In fact, Sinek's TED talk *Start With Why* covers the topic and is one of the most popular to date. "Communication is not about speaking what we think. Communication is about ensuring others hear what we mean." According to Sinek, this is a vital part of leadership.

Self-Motivation

"So in my mind, I was like, 'Okay, that means I have two years to open a bookstore.' I took responsibility for it." - Noelle Santos Owner, The Lit Bar

Simply put, when you're your own boss you have to be able to keep yourself motivated to work effectively and consistently. Entrepreneurs must be able to work through creative ruts and points of feeling uninspired to keep their businesses going. This starts with knowing what drives you to keep going and drawing upon necessary inspiration when motivation is low.

A great example of this is entrepreneur Noëlle Santos, who didn't intend to open a bookstore — she worked in HR for an IT firm — but was shaken by the news that the Barnes & Noble she frequented was closing.

The joy of reading was important to her, so she had to do something. "I was disgusted knowing that there was just one bookstore at the time. So that petition galvanized the property owners and Barnes & Noble and the politicians, and they came to an agreement that they would extend the lease for two years. So in my mind, I was like, 'Okay, that means I have two years to open a bookstore.' I took responsibility for it."

Dedicated to her mission, she even worked at other bookstores for free over the course of two and a half years to learn about the industry. From there, Santos fundraised and energized a community behind The Lit. Bar, bringing a bookstore back to the Bronx. The lesson here is that grit has to be inspired by something.

Confident

"Part of having a successful business is not just being able to perform, but making sure that everyone knows how well you are doing." - Monica Eaton-Cardone COO and Founder, Chargebacks911

If you have an idea you want to bring to life and share with others, you have to have the confidence to see it through. Whether you are introducing a new product to the market, or are seeking outside funding for your business, you must be able to speak to what you offer clearly and confidently. Successful entrepreneurs stand behind their ideas without letting concern over what others may think get in the way.

In an article on women entrepreneurs in tech, Monica Eaton-Cardone emphasizes the importance of confidence, even in the face of failure. "We fail our way to success. It means you had the courage to try and there's no way you can get to success without confronting failures." To Eaton-Cardone, failure isn't an obstacle to confidence, especially when it's so important for entrepreneurs to market themselves. Instead, failure can become a strength.

She encountered such failure herself on her journey to revolutionize solutions in payment processing, and such obstacles nearly caused her business to crumble. On her website, she says, "Instead of folding up shop, I decided to dig myself out of this pit ... I built an entire program based on every trial and error lesson I had learned — and it worked. Before long, the very same banks that had tried to shut down my business were calling and asking for my assistance."

Flexibility

To have a sustainable business and see long-term success, entrepreneurs must be willing to pivot when necessary. Whether it is reformulating a product to make it better, or revising a business strategy to remain competitive, entrepreneurs who are too rigid and afraid to embrace change are at a disadvantage.

When an entrepreneur is flexible in their approach, they are able to take advantage of new opportunities as they come which can pay off in the long run. Business owners who are slow to adapt to change can miss out on valuable opportunities to innovate and adapt to their customer's needs.

The lesson of flexibility is one that entrepreneur Hyungsoo Kim learned during the development of Eone's first product, a tactile wristwatch for the visually impaired. The first iteration of the watch relied on braille, didn't have a strong visual aesthetic appeal, and wasn't functional for non-visually impaired individuals.

During a focus group meeting, Kim and his team found out that their customers wanted a product that would be attractive and inclusive even for those who didn't have a visual impairment. This was something the design team hadn't considered, and they had to go back to the drawing board.

"After that meeting, our concept prototype literally went into the trash bin. We were building something that we thought they wanted basing on common misconceptions and stereotypes."

However, this lesson influenced their brand and its values. "We changed our name to Eone which is short for Everyone."

Risk-Taker

"To win big, you sometimes have to take big risks." - Bill Gates, Co-Founder, Microsoft

The ability to take a calculated risk is one of the most valuable skills an entrepreneur can have. When business owners are willing to take risks, they are able to learn valuable lessons in business that can help their company in the long run.

Taking risks also helps businesses find new ways to differentiate themselves from the competition, which is especially helpful in saturated markets. In the event the risk doesn't have the intended result, the entrepreneur can still apply the valuable lessons learned to future business decisions.

Microsoft's Bill Gates is credited with the quote, "To win big, you sometimes have to take big risks." Gates certainly took risks throughout the history of Microsoft, but perhaps his most notable risk was leaving Harvard during his sophomore year in 1975 to found the company. His vision was "a computer on every desk and in every home," which was something no one could have conceived of at the time. The risk he took to make that vision a reality paid off, and Microsoft is worth more than a Harvard degree.

Resilient

"When you've already experienced great challenges in your career, it gives minor setbacks a different perspective." - Kimberly Bryant Founder and CEO, Black Girls Code

Last but certainly not least, successful entrepreneurs must have a sense of resiliency. While running a business, it is common for entrepreneurs to face closed doors and to be told "no" often by potential customers and those they are seeking funding from.

Many entrepreneurs may find themselves starting multiple businesses if their initial idea doesn't take off. According to the

Bureau of Labor Statistics, nearly half of the small businesses fail within the first four years. Some successful business owners may find their first few business ideas weren't sustainable in the long run but can apply those learnings to new businesses. Whether an entrepreneur isn't granted a sale or opportunity or has to start at square one, being resilient and inventive in the face of challenges is a must.

Founder and CEO of Black Girls Code, Kimberly Bryant, encountered adversity along her career path as a Black woman in electrical engineering and biotechnology. It was when her daughter shared her interests in math and science that Bryant became a champion for STEM education for young girls of color. She founded her organization, Black Girls Code, and was originally met with opposition. In an interview with Shondaland Bryant details how "People did not want to fund something called Black Girls Code (BGC) — they would try to get us to change our name. Even the few organizations that were doing something similar didn't take us seriously."

These roadblocks didn't stop her, and she funded the organization with her own 401k. With perseverance and resilience, the organization gained steam and became a voice for social activism.

These traits along with a vision for what you want to accomplish are paramount to your success as an entrepreneur. Once you internalize your drive, you can then begin putting goals to paper and build out concrete action items to realize them.

Chapter 3

Innovation and Profit

LinkedIn, the world's largest professional network on the internet, has to say about an Entrepreneur: "An entrepreneur is someone who *locates the need of society* and tries to meet them *with an innovative idea.* On the other hand, entrepreneurship refers to the process of establishing a business entity, intending *to get profit as a return* in the future."

Two phrases are note-worthy here, and those phrases truly struck me: *"meet the need with an innovative idea,"* and *"get profit as a return".*

In this chapter let's learn why innovation is an inalienable aspect of entrepreneurship, what impact it does on those who innovate, and what it does to those who do not. Innovation is inseparable from the entrepreneur. It is a must-possess, a vital, and a strong aspect that can make or break the entrepreneur. If the entrepreneur handles the changes brought by innovation and successfully shapes his or her own business according to the changes of time, this surely breeds profit - which by the way, is not necessarily of monetary value. Read on.

Innovation: An Entrepreneur's Life Source

The classic cliché, "Change is the only thing constant in this world" is spot on. New ideas and methods are discovered every hour – big and small.

For entrepreneurs, innovation creates new opportunities but unfortunately, also means an end to another. So, what should an entrepreneur do to stay afloat? Simple. He or she should constantly innovate and drift along with the constant changes of time because the truth is, *innovation is a life source.*

Since January 2001, the beginning of the new millennium, the world witnessed the sudden emergence of all things automatic – cars, phones, household assistants, and talking devices. Technology brought us to an experience that generations before us would have not imagined happening – a replacement of old for new.

Typewriters were replaced with computers and tablets, traditional libraries have been replaced with the world wide web, and bulky telephones were replaced with hand-held devices. After the global Corona Virus (COVID-19) pandemic, face-to-face meetings were replaced by Zoom Conferences or "virtual meetings". Social media platform Facebook introduced Metaverse Technology where people can meet and discuss in an online space. Every day, the old is replaced by the new, and the world is constantly shaken – in a good way – by the convenience and breakthroughs brought by innovation.

In an article published by Northwestern University, America saw the loss of an average of two newspapers per week between late 2019 and May 2022, leaving an estimated 70 million people in places that are already news deserts and areas that are at high risk of becoming so. Prior to that steep decline, newspapers' weekday circulation had fallen by 7% and Sunday circulation by 4% in the United States, their greatest decline since 2010. If the trend continues, a third of newspapers will be lost by 2025.

In that research, the newspaper industry is indeed facing obsoletion. Couple that with the rising digitization, fed by the new methods introduced by the pandemic, the print news industry is required to "shape up or ship out". This is the primary reason why newspaper companies nowadays are left without choice to move toward the digital spaces – social media, online news sites, and YouTube – to bring the latest news and updates.

We conclude, therefore, that innovation – despite its benefits to humankind – can be both good and bad for an entrepreneur. Some businesses grow, but some businesses close because of the effects of innovation. With this trend, entrepreneurs need to constantly keep forecast the latest innovative ideas in their industry to survive.

According to an article from McKinsey and Company, published on their website:

John F. Kennedy once observed that the word "crisis" in Chinese is composed of two characters-one representing danger, and the other opportunity. He may not have been entirely correct on the linguistics, but the sentiment is true enough: a crisis presents a choice. This is particularly true today.

The COVID-19 pandemic has upended nearly every aspect of life, from the personal (how people live and work) to the professional (how companies interact with their customers, how customers choose and purchase products and services, and how supply chains deliver them). In our recent survey of more than 200 organizations across industries, more than 90 percent of executives said they expect the fallout from COVID-19 to fundamentally change the way they do business over the next five years, with almost as many asserting that the crisis will have a lasting impact on their customers' needs.

Jesus, Steve, and Innovation

The innovative minds of our two extreme entrepreneurs are without question. Extreme entrepreneurs as they are named, these two personalities have brought innovation to a high level – changing their generation and the generations that follow.

For Steve Jobs, he brought a milestone of technological innovation for competitors to duplicate. Steve did not merely create a "fixed innovative idea", he instead opened the doors of innovation for other brilliant minds to play and be creative with. It is like introducing an entirely new idea that breeds other big ideas but is still anchored on the original concept.

For example, Jobs' innovation of using touch screen technology for cellular phones did not cause a dead-end but rather paved the way for more innovations. It bred more concepts when competitors started to copy the functionality that Apple introduced and added features that bring new value to the touchscreen technology.

Jesus on the other hand, is without a doubt, a man of vision and innovation. Jesus' innovative mind was demonstrated in his various miracles performed with his disciples, and how he broke the ancient traditions and replaced them with new ones, shattering the archaic belief systems.

Customary to traditions at that time, the temples were the only places where rabbis taught and worshipped God. The synagogue was the place people gather for worship. But Jesus was innovative. He knew that the love of God is within each person, so he took God's teachings to the place where ordinary people gather.

Jesus now paved the way to a new concept of worship – the church is "within you" (Luke 17:21) – teaching that God's love is accessible – wherever and whenever He is needed. It opened a new wave of ideology – *God is not too far away.* He hears you when you ask. He forgives you when you repent. Ask and you shall receive. Knock and you shall be opened. And so on.

Today, these teachings are the fundamentals in Christianity – that the archaic ways of connecting to God's Kingdom are no longer through physical temples or buildings but through a personal connection to Him, only when one believes.

Profit with a Purpose

This chapter so far teaches us that innovation is essential for an entrepreneur. Efforts done in entrepreneurial innovation are for profitable purposes – meaning, there is an internal motivation for innovation. Commonly, it is for a certain profit. However, the definition of "profit" differs for every entrepreneur.

As entrepreneurs, we are all driven by our personal definition of profit. Profit drives us to wake up every morning and be innovative.

Let's ask ourselves. How do we visualize "profit"? Does your entrepreneurial soul call you for monetary profit? Are you driven by the soul to provide opportunities for people who are employed in your business? Are you driven by fame or international attention? Or are you like our extreme entrepreneurs who were driven by their souls to create a change in this world? There is definitely no right or wrong definition of profit.

However, if we look at the Bible, it speaks about profit beyond money and fortune – giving warnings of how we should acquire profit. The Bible speaks of a deeper sense of the word. This definition has brought entrepreneurs a shift from monetary profit to a *"profit with a purpose"*. In Mark 8:36, Jesus said to his disciples, "What good is it for someone to gain the whole world, yet forfeit their soul?"

Here, the Bible now teaches ethics and morals for businessmen to follow – never exchange your soul for monetary or worldly profits. The Bible warns us that it is worthless to forfeit our soul to gain the whole world. Here, we learn that we may have all the riches that this world can offer or obtain the attention of the world, but if we sold our souls to evil, we are worthless.

This powerful verse created a principle every entrepreneur must follow – building a business with a purpose. Jesus opened the eyes of entrepreneurs to caution themselves to keep their souls upright. Jesus taught the concept of *profit beyond life* – the soul will live on after it departs the body, leaving all worldly things behind. Jesus taught every entrepreneur a lesson for generations - build profits that last.

Chapter 4

Types of Entrepreneurs

Every online material or literature about entrepreneurship varies in terms of differentiating entrepreneurs. When searching the web, we see so many different types and variations. I believe we can differentiate them in simple terms.

But first, we should put to mind what makes entrepreneurs alike: Entrepreneurs can be in operation as a single individual gathering support from outside sources or involved in a multi-national operation in any endeavor, business, not-for-profit, social organization, or whatever operation imaginable. However, all entrepreneurs are not created equal. While all are soul-driven risk-takers, that is where the similarity stops.

To provide a simpler and clear-cut perspective, I will divide entrepreneurs into three types: basic, advanced, and extreme. Let's dive into each of those:

Basic Entrepreneur: *Improving What Exists*

Anyone who starts an operation is an entrepreneur. My lemonade stand was an entrepreneurial activity with a very short life—one day. The basic entrepreneur is one who opens a craft shop, starts a car repair, hangs out a professional shingle, or launches a restaurant. Basic entrepreneur reality is binary: *you survive or you don't*. The basic entrepreneur's quest is to survive and to profit from it. In all basic entrepreneur situations, the entrepreneur is taking an existing concept overlaid by her/his soul and improving on it.

One inspiring basic entrepreneur success story is Ray Kroc, who grew McDonald's restaurant from one location in 1957 to about 40,031 McDonald's restaurants (as of March 2023) in over 100 countries.

From the start, Kroc's goal was to have an empire using the franchise model to allow for rapid growth. While the number of restaurants was an important motivator for Kroc, each location had to make a profit, or his empire would fail. Each location required a net profit sufficient to support the franchisee and provide for continual improvements dictated by the franchisor. The management style had to be one of discipline at all levels such that the customer experience would be the same no matter which regional location was visited. Manuals and training covered all areas of operating a restaurant, from cleanliness to food preparation to physical layout. The tiny details are incorporated, thus, there is very little flexibility, if any at all, allowed from the contents of the manuals and training. The basic entrepreneur's (Ray Kroc) vision was to expand in the fast-food niche, and he did so on a grand scale.

My basic entrepreneurial experience was starting a direct marketing advertising agency in 1981. Like many agencies in that era, our communications realm included direct mail, print advertising, TV, package insert/take ones, and telemarketing. Our success or failure was dependent on how successfully we assisted our clients' successes. If we provided positive marketing results, we could live to provide more services in the future. If the results were not positive, we may not be reengaged for more services. I did nothing wildly different from my competitors as we were all using the same media in some combination, what did differ is the creative concepts we developed to produce results and the results we produced.

Advanced Entrepreneur: Push for Greater

Advanced entrepreneurs use existing technologies, systems, or processes in innovative ways to leverage their business beyond basic entrepreneur.Jeff Bezos' Amazon is an example of an advanced entrepreneur. Starting as an online bookseller in 1994, he has taken the mail order concept to the internet and morphed it into several businesses. Books expanded to music and eventually, to all manner of products that are inventoried and shipped from multiple warehouses. One new business leverages online technology and systems that run Amazon leased as a service to other businesses to run their operations. Another business sells other company's products from their inventory using Amazon marketing and systems for which Amazon receives a percentage of sales.

For many years, the measurement of Amazon's success was gross sales, much to the chagrin of Wall Street. Profits, if there were any, were a by-product of operations that were plowed back into the business for more expansion. Of late profits have begun to pile up but are still a by-product of ongoing ventures into food sales, retail, health care, delivery, and many other opportunities that we have yet to know about. The management style of the advanced entrepreneur is aggressive as venturing into such far-afield markets require an ever-advancing set of visions, operations, and technology.Today, Amazon is one of the largest "cloud" computer service providers in the world. Providing cloud computing is totally different from online consumer retail selling. While Bezos provided the entrepreneur, he has obviously added many thousands of people to perform the production, administration, and integration of his multiple businesses and endeavors.

My advanced entrepreneur decision occurred in 1994. At that time, my agency was providing new customer acquisition programs for a major computer company. One program was a series of seminars about how to access this new technology called the internet. I attended the first seminar in the area. What I saw was the future of direct marketing communications. I was fully committed, so I started another company to provide website development, database interface with online access, and website hosting. My existing agency client base became my internet development clients virtually overnight, so my expansion was off and running.

So excited was I with this new communication technology that I packed up a couple of techies and equipment and went to the 1994 Direct Marketing Association International Conference as an exhibitor. At that conference, one leading mail order catalog consultant took a look at the concept and said, "It (the internet) will never go anywhere in the mail order industry." Amazon, for one, proved his prediction incorrect. I sold the internet company in 2000 for two reasons: first, I was traveling all the time consulting, and second, running a technology-centric company as a non-technologist was in my consulting (and personal) opinion, nuts.

Extreme Entrepreneurs: Shakers of the System

This category of entrepreneurs is populated with very few individuals. The goal of extreme entrepreneurs is to provide people with new experiences. They measure themselves by acceptance of their concept. Their vision is to change the world, and they don't really care if they make any money. Day by day, extreme entrepreneurs strive to steer the wheel away from its current direction – to go out of the norms, standards, and current belief systems. The extreme entrepreneur shakes the system, upsets the status quo, and in the end, brings something new to the table – something that transforms lives.

One such individual is Walt Disney. He built a world of entertainment with an animated mouse captaining a steamboat as its cornerstone. He turned the Coney Island-type amusement parks of the day into a destination entertainment park when he opened Disneyland in 1955. Disney parks and resorts, according to their website, are six world-class vacation destinations with twelve theme parks and fifty-two resorts that "are making memories that last a lifetime." According to Andrew Beattle, Investopedia, Oct 2018,

"Walt Disney is one of the most powerful companies, in one of the most powerful sectors of any economy: entertainment."

Before my entrepreneurial days, I had an opportunity to work with the Disney organization to manufacture figures of Disney characters for sale in their gift shops. I recall the character standards book as a massive document showing every character from every angle. A few of the rules:

Mickey Mouse, Minnie Mouse, Goofy, and Donald Duck always wear gloves with three fingers and a thumb. The mouse ears are never shown in the profile they are always full-on, front or back.

Four decades later is a long time to remember such details, but it was so impressive and specific that there was no leeway in representing any of the characters exactly as had been the case since its creation in 1928. This illustrates the extreme entrepreneur's attention to details that deliver the desired experiences.

Today, Disney is a force in the entertainment industry and is forever embarked in each of the lives of children and *children at heart*. Disney continues to bring its unmatched brand to all of its theme parks, songs, movies, and even to its merchandise, much so that when people see an image of its logo or icon, people *feel the experience*. Disney successfully took the world to an emotional connection beyond the physical connection.

Taking into account all of these, we conclude: extreme entrepreneurs are way too different than those entrepreneurs that we have come to know. Extreme entrepreneurs have characteristics that truly set them apart from the other two kinds – they go beyond the boundaries of entrepreneurship, bringing with them new concepts that create a new set of ways, ideas, and beliefs.

An Entrepreneur's Soul

Parsing entrepreneurs into three groups is intended to illustrate that all entrepreneurs are not equal. Jeff Bezos and I both embraced the internet in 1994 with businesses started using the technology. He is now one of the richest men in the world, and

I am writing about it. His goal was to leverage the technology as a mail-order company. My goal was to provide clients with a virtually free marketing communications medium. His application of the medium eclipsed all other mail-order companies. I was eclipsed by the wave of web developers and do-it-yourself web technologies. The Direct Marketing Association is now the Data Marketing Association reflecting the marriage of communications and data collection. This transformation tells you something about the amount of customer and prospect information that is gathered through the internet. Every browser activity can be stored and analyzed, from purchases to previews with no purchase. But this is fodder for a different book.

The soul of the entrepreneur is a watermark on any size venture. It expresses itself through the people it attracts as customers and as employees. In the case of a franchise operation, where the deliverable is defined by the franchisor, the type of people the entrepreneur hires expresses her/his soul through their interactions with customers. The franchisee sets the example and standards, wittingly or not. A simple example is a smile instead of a smirk, a tone set by the franchise owner. A grumpy owner develops grumpy employees, which doesn't bode well for customer service.

Steve Jobs's hiring profile was to hire hard-working, intelligent people, not functional specialists. He actually had poor results, hiring based on resume experience. The hiring practice included putting a candidate in front of whatever technology was being developed and seeing their reactions. No excitement and wonderment by the applicant, no hire. People, whose souls were attracted by his concept and idea, expressed through the products, were essential to Apple's success. Jobs's attitude was smart people can figure things out regardless of their past experience. So one's success at Apple was in one's hands. All employees were "on board" with a critical expectation of perfection that survives today, years after Steve Jobs's death. Apple is one of the largest companies in the world today.

Jesus Christ had twelve immediate "employees" known as his disciples. These were twelve ordinary men complemented by a couple of women followers. None were from the established Jewish Levites. He picked men who would be good disciples to become good apostles, with the charge to carry His message throughout the world. Eleven disciples shared their souls with Jesus and came to understand their mission after Pentecost, the coming to them of the Holy Spirit. Each would carry both teachings and interpretations sufficiently enough to change people from fear to love. So successful were they that Christianity has over two billion followers making up about 31.5% of the world population according to PBS Learning Media.

Each type of entrepreneur had to find *like souls*. Ray Kroc had to find souls that could thrive under his rules, which he did quite successfully. Jeff Bezos had to find souls that could adopt his vision and then operate in each business successfully. Steve Jobs needed to have capable people whose souls understood his need to put technology in the hands of everyone to their delight and enjoyment. Jesus Christ had to have souls that could, through their souls, communicate love as an alternative lifestyle to fear.

From here on, we will focus just on the extreme entrepreneur. Not to say this is a superior type of entrepreneur, rather it is the most difficult to understand. It is the most complex of all entrepreneurs and only a few belong to such a category. It is the type of entrepreneur who stands out, and whose soul is different from others.

Chapter 5

Extreme Entrepreneurs

In the previous chapter, we parsed entrepreneurs into three categories: basic, advanced, and extreme. Parsing them into categories gives us a more in-depth understanding of what an extreme entrepreneur really is, providing us with a better foundation for the study of the two personalities, Steve Jobs and Jesus Christ.

Each had a soul that drove their vision to change the world. They fit into the category of extreme entrepreneurs as they have shaken the system, providing concepts that created a *new set of ways, ideas, and beliefs* for the world in their respective years of existence. Let us explore these comparatively.

In this chapter, I will fall back on my undergraduate degree in philosophy. Just understanding the traits of an entrepreneur isn't sufficient to understand the metaphysics or philosophy associated with the extreme entrepreneur.

Philosophy deals with the hard-to-answer or deep questions about humanity—our metaphysical being, including our physical being. To ask questions like, what makes us take risks or why should we love a vision of beauty and elegance more than the people who help us bring that vision to reality or where is the line between earth and heaven? It is to ask questions that philosophers have spent centuries talking about. At this point, we will uncouple from characteristics and traits into the metaphysical arena of the extreme entrepreneur.

What makes extreme entrepreneurs special is their point of reference. To explain this, we will explore Plato's divided line as explained in *The Republic,* written sometime around 500 BC. In part, the line is divided into two major categories: physical and intelligible. See Figure 1.

In the physical world, we are dealing with physical objects. In Plato's metaphor, the visible world has two levels: images and objects. Learning begins with images, pictures in books, or on cave walls; often supported by verbal explanations. For example, an image of a tree provides sufficient information so that when we see an actual tree, we know what it is. Another example is a square illustrated on a piece of paper. As it is already an object but if we take a picture of the object, the picture is a recognizable image. This illustrates that in the visible world, the process can move between the object and the image in either direction.

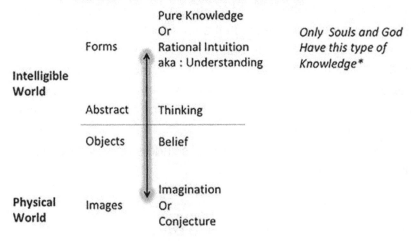

Plato's Divided Line

Pure Knowledge
Or
Only Souls and God
Forms   Rational Intuition   *Have this type of*
aka : Understanding *Knowledge**

Intelligible World

Abstract   Thinking

Objects   Belief

Imagination
Physical World   Images   Or
Conjecture

- * Quizlet.com Plato's Divided Line

Figure 1

Moving from the physical world to the intelligible world, the square would move from an object to a definition: a square is a two-

35

dimensional object with four equal sides and four 90-degree corners. The definition differentiates the square from a two-dimensional object with three sides and three 60-degree angles, a triangle. Our thought processes provide us the ability to make the differentiation without the benefit of any visual representation.

Plato asserts that the definitions of a square exist with or without our understanding of it. He referred to this level as "forms," which are to become the essence of our extreme entrepreneurs. Both Steve Jobs and Jesus Christ had a form that was in their respective souls. Their entrepreneurial challenge was to translate for us to understand how each makes our lives more magical and meaningful. The content of their souls was a priori, prior to experience. In both cases, there did not exist a reality from which they learned. They were guided by their souls that contained what they and only they knew.

In Figure 1, forms can be understood by our souls and God. This graphic and explanation came from an online educational site, Quizlet.com. (As hard as I tried, I could not find this Quizlet.com deck a second time or who created it, but I am profoundly appreciative of it as it supported my thesis on the soul that we will discuss further in later chapters).Typical learning starts with the physical world and moves up to the intelligible. For most of us, learning stops at the abstract or thinking level. However, for some, learning does rise to understanding or forms. Albert Einstein's theory of relativity revolutionized physics.

His theories came from his soul's understanding, as there was no a priori work for him to study.

Jobs and Jesus: Technology and Love

For extreme entrepreneurs, their souls had the forms, the understanding a priori, and it was their task to bring it down the line to us to levels that we can understand. Both Jobs and Jesus lived with a complete understanding of the task of humanizing what they innately knew.

In both cases, the challenges were the same, converting what their souls directed them into an executable reality. Each had to move the unknown into an ignorant world, toward a world that makes sense of it all.Jobs's soul envisioned common people having beneficial control of technology to serve as the "bicycle for the mind," as Steve Jobs put it. He adapted the GUI (graphical user interface) into metaphorical graphics and gave us point-and-click simplicity for selection. These adaptations allowed the everyday person to use the underlying technology without any programming experience. The inclusion of technology did not get in the way of life, as had been the case until his innovations made life more magical.

Christ's soul, on the other hand, had the mission to lay the foundation for humankind to understand who we are, how to live together, and how to have happiness here on earth couched not in fear but in love.

The world He saw was totally contra to what existed at the time. People were fearful of not living up to the expectations and rules of religious leaders. They were fearful of the Roman army and control structure from Rome. Fear was the currency of the day. Through His three-year ministry, Jesus demonstrated how love was a better currency than fear, and He demonstrated what he taught. For example, Christ told the people to love their neighbor as themselves and this meant Romans and church leaders as well. He taught people to love the unlovable as magnified by his choice of disciples – these were people that society scorned during those times. His choice was unconventional: one was a zealot, one was a thief, and one was a tax collector. The rest were commoners, unpopular in society.

Adding to this, the scriptures tell us even His disciples were skeptical of where their leader was leading them. Jesus espoused an unpopular belief or practice that if it ever happened today, would turn out to be viral social media content. His ways were non-traditional and pushed the boundaries of norms. He shook the system.

But love was Jesus's teaching foundation. His life taught people to accept sinners and that forgiveness is freely available for everyone who is willing to repent – regardless of the weight of their sins or their social background.

His concept of humans was that of individuals free to love and be loved. He communicates to us using "parable puzzles," short stories that can have endless interpretations. Stories about how a grain of yeast can make bread rise represent the kingdom of God. Or how a wayward son who scandalizes his father's good name is forgiven.

The parable of the Good Samaritan is universal in its appeal and interpretations. Through parables, Jesus's word can be as metaphysical as it is practical.

Chapter 6

People or Things

I spent several years as a state representative. My first year in the House of Representatives was a learning curve that went straight up. It became extremely obvious that legislators legislate. We file bills to add new laws and/or amend or delete existing laws. This process requires a mountain of reading and rereading when amendments are added. The confusing part was that seasoned legislators talked in shorthand and leveraged their knowledge of past legislation. After a couple of years, it became obvious that many bill topics are revisited every new two-year term to undo or redo existing law. So over time, many topics are revisited and therefore, not requiring so much learning.

Since the first-year, learning curve was so steep so I decided to converse with senior reps to determine where the survival handrails and lifelines reside. In one of these conversations, one senior rep said, "People or things," that's always the decision. Where does the state spend its revenues (taxes, fees, and fines) most effectively, at least in each legislator's mind. Is the priority on state employees' salaries and benefits, public education, and/or citizen services? Or are roads, bridges, and trucks a better use of funds? The answer to all options is—yes.

Both people and things are important. On further evaluation of the people or things categorization, it became clear that funding for things often affects people. For example, new state police cars and equipment could bring the average speed down on interstate highways due to more or better enforcement of speed limits. Driver behavior is modified because there are more things. However, hiring more state police could have the same effect.

So the decision is, which is a better use of funds: improved equipment or more state police? From the state police point of view, both are important and that's where legislating gets tough. Is lowering the average speed on the interstate more important than reducing deaths from drugs? Is the thing called average speed more important than the people who are dying from overdoses? And so it goes for lawmakers, *people or things*.

Extreme Entrepreneurs: People or Things

The two extreme entrepreneurs this book exposes had two different souls. Steve Jobs brought forth products to the delight of customers. Jesus Christ brought forth a new way to approach, evaluate, and live in this world, to humankind's delight. These are not mutually exclusive as we will see.

Establishing the dichotomy based on *people or things* to our two extreme entrepreneurs makes it easy for us to understand their persona. Steve Jobs is 100 percent focused on things, Apple Products, with demonstrably no concern for people on an interpersonal basis. He was concerned about customer experiences using Apple products, and anyone who did not share his vision cannot ride his boat. His passions and frequent confrontations drove his employees to achieve results beyond their own expectations. Steve Jobs was the leader of Apple that delivered what his soul directed, *bicycles for the mind.*

Jesus Christ, on the other hand, is 100 percent focused on people with no interest in things or the material world. His charge was to redirect humankind from external rules and forces that create fear as the foundation and guiding principle for humanity, instead directing them to themselves and relationships with others and God. His soul provided the perfect role model for his followers and us. Loving everyone he came in contact with, even when the social norms would indicate otherwise.

When Jesus asked us to "love your neighbor as yourself," it magnified his priority on people. He did not have a necessity for any things to complement his request. He loathed idolatry and excoriated the commercialization of the synagogue. He also expanded the concept of neighbor to include all people, friends, and foes alike. Anyone who took the time to learn of Jesus's teachings knew they were loved and should love. Love is to humans what water is to fish. Love is all around us – and Christ showed us exactly what love can do through the very end of his life – His death on the cross.**People, Things, and Both**

A final analysis of people and things, however, is that entrepreneurs who concentrate on things are also often developing things for people. In Steve Jobs' world, Apple products were developed to improve the experiences and capabilities of people. Investment in infrastructure things is to ultimately improve citizens' lives, too.For example, my church receives Christmas gift requests through what we called, the Salvation Army. Clearly, the gift requests are things, clothing, and toys. However, the members who buy and wrap the gifts are not doing it for the "thing" of it. They are doing it because there are children receiving the gift whose lives will be a little happier. The things are an expression of each member's love.

Things can have an enormous impact on people. It can improve lives, it can bring happiness and comfort like how those flowers offered to a grieving family who lost a member deliver emotional comfort.

While it is true that material things of this world do fade, we can deduce from the previous examples this fact: The way we view "things" have a great significance in our lives. Are we engrossed with the benefits that the things of this world offer to us? Or are we engrossed in using the things of this world to create a significant change for other people? If we chose the latter, it only meant that we have successfully combined the mindset of our two extreme entrepreneurs.

Yin and Yang and its Significance

Yin and Yang (Figure 1) is an icon that represents an ancient Chinese philosophy about the relationship of opposites – dark and light, male and female, people and things. As the Chinese philosophy taught, it is the interactions of these opposites that influence the results we experience or realize.

Steve Jobs and Jesus Christ are separated by two thousand years, so only we, Apple-era individuals who are Christians, can experience the benefits of their yin and yang.

Our present generation reaps the levels of comfort from the technology of Apple, at the same time, it also reaps the benefits of what Christians call the "grace period" – meaning, we live in a generation where there is an opportunity for free salvation, only if we believe in Him and accept Jesus as our Lord and Savior. We no longer need to labor for it, or pay the debt caused by our sins – it is offered for free through His grace.

Imagine, it is never too late to experience using an Apple product. By the same token, it is never too late to experience life's joys and salvation offered by Jesus.

Figure 1

The soul of each individual can have an effect of the perception of "things." A very good example of this is the story of the three stone masons constructing a new church. The masons were asked what they were doing.

The first said, "I am building a brick wall."

The second said, "I am building a church."

The third said, "I am building a magnificent structure where people will glorify the name of God!"

You see, all three masons were doing the same thing, but their souls brought them to different conclusions. Among the three masons, who do you think delivered the best results? I would speculate that each stone mason had different levels of job satisfaction accordingly.

For our extreme entrepreneurs, their motivation was not on "things". Steve Jobs devoted himself to, "putting a dent in the universe." His soul was far beyond most minds and visions, it could be said that he danced to a different drummer. Jesus Christ endeavored to replace a life of fear with a life of love and not just for Jews, but for all humanity, helping each person know they have God's love within their souls.

Extreme Entrepreneurs: Money and Fame

One thing both entrepreneurs have in common is their disinterest in the thing called money.

Income, profit, and disposable cash were never the drivers for our extreme entrepreneurs. All of their energies were devoted to their calling, their motivation, and their personal missions. We can learn something from them, a focus on money does not add to one's success. Just as sports players cannot fixate on the scoreboard, lest their sports endeavors suffer from divided attention, extreme entrepreneurs' souls always keep the main thing, the main thing. Their eyes were set on their chosen enterprise but they were not driven by monetary gain.

Matthew 6:19-21 exposes what Jesus thinks about monetary wealth: "Do not store up riches for yourselves here on earth, where moths and rust destroy, and robbers break in and steal. Instead, store up riches for yourselves in heaven, where moths and rust cannot destroy, and robbers cannot break in and steal. For your heart will always be where your riches are." Another verse in the New Testament says, "For the love of money is the root of all evil: which while some coveted after, they have erred from the faith, and pierced themselves through with many sorrows." (1 Timothy 6:10)

It is apparent in this verse that Jesus never had any interest in money. He was more interested in investing for spiritual wealth that can neither be broken nor destroyed.

Extreme Entrepreneurs: On Society's Perception

Another commonality that our extreme entrepreneurs have is their disinterest in what society perceives of them. They did not seek recognition, titles, or accolades. They do not want to be praised for a good job.

When Steve Jobs started a *"think different"* internal campaign he said: *"Here's to the crazy ones, the misfits, the rebels, the troublemakers, the round pegs in the square holes... the ones who see things differently—they're not fond of rules, and they have no respect for the status quo. You can quote them, disagree with them, glorify or vilify them, but the only thing you can't do is ignore them because they change things. They push the human race forward, and while some may see them as the crazy ones, we see genius, because the people who are crazy enough to think that they can change the world, are the ones who do."*

Now, we see a glaring commonality between Jobs and Jesus. Both had an unconventional approach toward the achievement of goals. Both believed that the misfits, rebels, and troublemakers are those that make a difference in the world. You see, in Jesus' time, he had a non-traditional set of disciples – commoners, sinners, and those that society thinks incapable of being given a higher calling.

In fact, in many Bible stories, we learn that Jesus calls the most insignificant minority to take on the tasks: those who are hardly noticed, the most unqualified, and the reluctant.

Chapter 7

Soul

In preparation for exploring the achievements of our extreme entrepreneurs, it is necessary to lay a foundation for what both had in common. In the previous chapter, we learned that Steve and Jesus had two extreme differences: one lived a life centered on things; the other centered on people. But we also learned that as a human being, you have the power to impact *people* through *things*.

We have discussed that the extreme entrepreneurs' inspiration came not from this world or a priori (prior to experience). But once they had the inspiration, it now gives rise to these questions: Where was this inspiration kept and nurtured? What drove them each day to stay focused? What was the driver to motivate their actions?

As we all know, both extreme entrepreneurs have made a lasting impression on humankind, but the common main driver for both of them was this one aspect – their soul. In this chapter, we will uncover the soul of each of our main characters. As discussed at the beginning of this book, the soul is the compass however, it can be deceptive. Thus, one needs to obtain a discerning mind that balances the directions of the soul.

Steve Jobs and the Soul

Steve Jobs and Jesus Christ spoke of the soul in different ways. Jobs referred to the soul in his speech to Stanford University commencement speech in 2005, as quoted in "Think Like Steve Jobs":Your time is limited, so don't waste it living someone else's life. Don't be trapped by dogma—which is living with the results of other people's thinking. Don't let the noise of others' opinions drown out your own inner voice. *And most important, have the courage to follow your heart and intuition. They somehow already know what you truly want to become.* Everything else is secondary. (Emphasis added)In this passage, his reference to "follow your heart and intuition" is saying to follow your soul as "they somehow already know what you truly want to become." Jobs was, in my estimation, speaking about his own experience and belief as there is no doubt about his wanting to "put a dent in the universe." The most valuable message, to me, is, "Your time is limited, so don't waste it living someone else's life." This is Jobs's admonition to each of us, to follow the path that our soul or "inner voice" tries to direct each of us.

Jobs spoke from experience and from his philosophy of life. His belief set was innate. However philosophical and profound his message was and is, he will always be known for his magical products that continue to enhance human's use of technology. It cannot be stressed enough that Steve Jobs's creations came forth from his very soul.

Jesus Christ and the Soul

Jesus also had a set of innate beliefs; however, his beliefs were shared with God. Jesus also knew that the soul of each living thing contains a piece of the Divine, of God, the Creator. As explained by Richard Rohr, and as written at the beginning of this book:*"Our unique little bit of heaven is installed by the Manufacturer within the product, at the beginning! We are given a span of years to discover it, to choose it, and to live our own destiny to the full. If we do not, our True Self will never be offered again, in our unique form."*

47

Jesus also taught that love was the key to allowing our soul to express itself and usher us into our destiny through things or people.

In the Bible, Jesus said: *"Love the Lord your God with all your heart and with all your soul and with all your mind."* (Matthew 22)

This passage frames the triad: mind, body, and soul so specifically that we will look at each element in relation to the other and evaluate the interplay. For purposes of this discussion, we will include all living things: plants, animals, and humans. This is based on an online article by Richard Rohr:I think of the soul as anything's ultimate meaning which is held within. *Soul is the blueprint inside of every living thing that tells it what it is and what it can become.* When we meet anything at that level, we will respect, protect, and love it. (Emphasis added)

Adopting Richard Rohr's definition of the soul opens new dimensions for consideration.

The three parts of us that Jesus included:

1. *Mind. All sentient beings have a mind that provides a set of cognitive faculties including consciousness, imagination, perception, thinking, judgment, language, and memory, as well as autonomic systems that work in the background to keep our heart pumping and our process systems functioning. We generally ascribe the mind to the brain.*
2. *Body. The physical form that carries around our mind and soul, which allows us to move, communicate, hear, see, feel, smell; to function.*
3. *Soul. The intangible that makes us who we are as people, animals, or plants. It is the force that moves us to action, the arbiter of emotions, the source of inspiration, the hesitation or bounce in our step, the scale that keeps us in balance, and the voice that keeps us motivated or not. According to John Ortberg in Soul Keeping, your soul is your "youness." Richard Rohr, in Falling Upward, says, "Your soul has many secrets. They are only revealed to*

those who want them and are never completely forced on us."

Mind, Body, and Soul: Explained

To put mind, body, and soul in perspective, let's set up a Venn diagram (Figure 1). The mind is one circle. The body is another equally-sized circle beside the mind. Around both circles is a larger circle that is the soul. If the mind (non-autonomic) is lost, the body can still function. If the body is incapacitated, the mind can still function. If both the mind and body cease functioning, the being can still "live" as long as the soul survives.

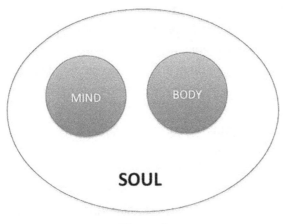

Figure 1

I have experienced this latter case. My mother had a series of strokes that robbed her of her mind and the use of her body. Nourishment was provided by a feeding tube, which kept her "alive" as her autonomic systems functioned, as always, without her willing them to. Her soul prevailed. However, after about two years of non-communication, non-aware, immobile "life," nourishment was withheld, eventually causing death by depriving the autonomic system of the elements to continue to support the soul. Only then did her soul cease to be part of her being.

So what happens to the soul when it departs a body? If the soul is the piece of Divine in each of us placed there by the manufacturer, like the manufacturer, it is eternal. Plato believed that the soul leaves the body to reside on a star as an unborn child. Christians believe that the soul goes to heaven to be with the manufacturer. Several Asian religions believe that the soul is reborn in another life form, hopefully human. No one really knows what happens when our soul leaves our body. When it does, then we will know. Or will we?

You will notice in the definition of the soul are included plants and animals, not just humans. This is a result of reading a work by Richard Rohr, *The Universal Christ*, where this assertion is explained. Adopting Richard Rohr's definition of the soul opens new dimensions for consideration, greatly expanding the function and opportunity the soul provides.

Using Figure 1 as it applies to a plant. There is a body that operates on an autonomic system, there is no mind, but there can certainly be a soul. The plant soul carries out the mission of the plant to survive and thrive. However, if environmental circumstances are not favorable and there is insufficient water or earth nutrients or any number of negative circumstances, the plant will die and along with it the plant's soul.

More important is the attraction of the plant soul and the human soul. There are some of us, me not among this group, who love to grow plants of beauty, plants of function, and plants for nourishment. During the growing season, these gardeners seem to be attracted to each other, comparing notes on how their various types of plants are doing. For me, the enjoyment is the abundance of cucumbers and tomatoes available when the growing season has been successful. One person I know spends all summer tending to a garden that brings forth a harvest that she cans (I don't know why it is called canning when the foods are stored in jars). One enjoyment of her soul is the growing and canning of the harvest that she uses for Christmas presents. Generally speaking, I am a failure at gardening. I attribute this to a soul that does not find fulfillment in gardening.

However, we do have a fern that was given to us by my wife's grandmother, who told us that the original fern came to the United

States via Canada from Sweden in the 1890s. Watered weekly and allowed a few hours of sun daily, this fern needs to be split and repotted once each year. The pots are large on the floor with rollers-type pots, so repotting is a production. The net result is that I get backed up every couple of years with too many of these potted plants, that I happily give away.

This is my admission that I do have an attachment to this perpetual fern. From time to time, when we were overwhelmed, I did discard a part or two when repotting, which, I dare say, made me sad. At the time, I had no idea there was any soul attraction.

Now, I understand. This leads us to the next chapter.

Chapter 8

Soul Powers

Your soul has a power beyond your imagination. While most of us limit the definition of the soul as "spirit" (or that which is eternal or transcends life on earth) there is more energy, power, and influence that we can utilize from our souls. The soul is broad in definition and it is just important that we learn each of its potential for us to tap into its influence and benefits.

The concept of the soul's influence on our lives is not a new concept. In Plato's *Republic,* Plato described the three parts of the soul— appetites, spirit, and mind.

According to Dr. Tom Kerns, North Seattle Community College, Philosophy 101 Online Course, the three are described as:

The first one, appetites, which include all our myriad desires for various pleasures, comforts, physical satisfactions, and bodily ease. There are so many of these appetites that Plato does not bother to enumerate them, but he does note that they can often be in conflict even with each other.

The second is the spirited or hot-blooded, part, i.e., the part that gets angry when it perceives (for example) an injustice being done. This is the part of us that loves to face and overcome great challenges, the part that can steel itself to adversity, and that loves victory, winning, challenge, and honor. (Note that Plato's use of the term *spirited* here is not the same as "spiritual." He means "spirited" in the same sense that we speak of a high-spirited horse, for example, one with lots of energy and power.)

The third is the mind (*nous*), our conscious awareness. This is the part of us that thinks, analyzes, looks ahead, rationally weighs options, and tries to gauge what is best and truest overall.

In *The Power of Soul,* by Dr. Zhi Gang Sha, the author offers many characteristics of the soul.

Your soul has conscience and intelligence. It learns. Your soul has emotion. Your soul has incredible wisdom. Your soul can communicate with other souls naturally. Your soul connects with your mind. Your soul can also reward you or give you warnings.

In this chapter, let's dive deep into the various powers of your soul and how your soul can connect with the living things around you.

The Soul Attractions

One great starting point is the attraction you have with your partner or spouse, especially if you refer to it as "love at first sight," which is often used to describe a magical moment in many of our lives. It is the feeling when your soul is magnetized to another. I attribute this moment to the fulfillment of our soul in all three parts of Plato's definition: *appetite, spirit, and mind.* We later refer to our spouse as our "soul mate," further recognizing a shared attraction that we have difficulty putting into words.

Having a soulmate, therefore, means having someone who mirrors your soul. Your appetites, your spirit, and your mind connect. It is like connecting a charger to a socket that brings energy and allows the equipment to work according to its function.

At this point, it is time to deviate and to recognize that our soul has many attributes that may improve our lives, and it also has an overwhelming attribute that truly brings richness to life—attractions of many types. Existing in a dimension beyond our understanding, our soul can be attracted to another soul, not just a spouse, and vice versa. This attraction is explained as, "birds of a feather flock together." What follows incorporates attraction at many levels as part of our soul. Figure 1 is a simple representation of this attraction.

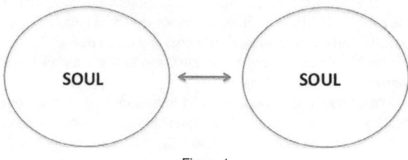

Figure 1

This kind of attraction, however, is not limited to *human and human.* Another attraction is between human and animal souls, pets. Animals of all ilk have a mind and body with an overarching soul. The bond with a pet transcends owning a living object. In fact, many people would rather be with their pets than with other humans. Do you have a pet that you are spiritually attracted to?

Soul attraction to plants is also possible. Such brings comfort and satisfaction. Soul attraction to pets can bring lifted spirits and happiness. Failure to thrive both plants and animals, bring some level of sadness and perhaps even despair to us humans. However, the soul attraction of other humans is the most rewarding and/or devastating attraction of all.

Figure 2

Figure 2 illustrates soul attractions at various levels. At the center of the world is our soul, which John Ortberg refers to as our "youness."

Our next level of soul attraction is with family. The primary family relationship is the spouse where the term, *soul mate,* is often used to describe the relationship. I can certainly relate. I met my wife when we were seventeen and instantly knew that she was the "one" for me, and happily, she felt the same way. We married four years later and will celebrate fifty-three years of marriage this year. Family relationships are a mixed bag that ranges from close to strained, but it is founded in shared souls through marriage or blood. In discussing adult children with my friends, there are situations where there is attraction and rejection at the same time. We share soulful love with our children but may not want to be around them.

The next souls are the souls of our friends. Here we can have friends who are like family. We can also have friends that range from associates to acquaintances. Our connections with these people are often through work or some common interests.

The outer reaches of our soul relationships are with various communities. Speaking for myself, many of my friends, at many levels, are in the community at church. There are other communities of which I am part where the soul connection has never developed. I am a fifty-year member of a fraternal organization I joined because my father and grandfather were members. While I understand the *why and what* of the organization intellectually, my soul has never wanted to be active in the organization. I am also a member of a veteran's organization where my participation is minimal. I have decided it is my duty to support the organization with my dues.

But my soul has the same level of attraction as I had with military service. Even though I grew up as an "Army brat" and went through ROTC to begin a life as a career soldier, my soul did not connect with the organization. I have served as a member of my town's planning board for a couple of decades – a service that my soul wants to pursue just as I am compelled to serve as a state legislator for the outstanding compensation of $100 per year.

One confusing community was my college fraternity. For the first three years of my college career, the fraternity was the most important group of guys and the only group of guys I wanted to be around. We all had some soul connection fulfilled by the community. In the summer of my junior year, I married my soul mate, and in my senior year, I could have cared less about being around the brothers. I have been back to one fraternity homecoming, arriving on Friday evening and almost instantly couldn't wait until departure on Sunday.

Getting updates on careers and challenges were interesting, but I have no interest in ever doing it again. That time, my soul's energy was more drawn to my wife, my new family. Thus the soul attraction may also change its course over time.Of course, when there are soul attractions, Yin and Yang indicate that the opposite must be true as well. We can also have rebuff or rejection, too. This is where Jesus's guidance is most effective. He said, "Love your neighbor as yourself."

Going back to Figure 2, you are in the center of your world, and loving yourself must be a starting point. You must love your *"youness."* If you don't, this might be an indication that you are not letting your soul be your Jiminy Cricket (the cartoon character that provided the puppet Pinocchio with advice). We can have a rejection of a group because of a variety of reasons, which we will discuss in a later chapter. But know that both attraction and rejection are governed by your soul and communicated to you for your own good. Use it.

As we end this chapter, ask yourself: Which part of my soul has the power to influence? Whose soul is my soul is attracted to and how can I strengthen this attraction? How can I utilize the power of my soul?

Chapter 9

Steve Jobs

Dubbed "the charismatic pioneer of the personal computer era," and the visionary genius behind the leading phone manufacturer in the world, Steve Jobs took cellular phone technology to a different level.

Even after his death on October 5, 2011 (due to respiratory arrest related to a tumor) and with his great contribution to technology, many people still know little about this extreme entrepreneur's life, and how he placed a "dent in the universe" through his driver – his soul. From a singular concept to the world's most valuable brand. How did Steve Jobs rise to fame and power?

Steve Jobs was adopted at birth, and raised by a blue-color family in the San Francisco area. He went to college and dropped out after the first semester. Steve stayed on campus for another year, auditing classes that interested him, followed by a trip to India. The 1970s was the era of Maharishi Mahesh Yoga, transcendentalism, and meditation (you may go to the source and check it out). On his return after seven months, he changed his appearance – shove his head and wore Indian traditional clothing. Soon after, Steve took a job at Hewlett-Packard where he was involved in the base production of computers.At that time, computers filled entire rooms with raised floors, so water could be circulated inside the systems to keep them cool. Information was stored on magnetic tape with a fixed record length and linear access – things young people nowadays will certainly cringe thinking about. Luckily, I experienced this firsthand. In the late '70s, I was employed by the Boy Scouts of America with the charge to launch the BSA into the mail-order business. My task was simple: send each member a catalog of the BSA merchandise. There was only one problem. The information about members was organized by packs, troops, and posts, not a home address. What was required was to match a member number with that member number's home address, create a new file, and then print mailing labels. No big deal. Right?

The processing took the IBM mainframe computers six days to process the five million records. During this time, the headquarters data processing came to a standstill, which included printing paychecks for National Council personnel. Needless to say, I was not a very popular member of the HQ team. When the IT staff delivered three pallets of labels to my office, I knew it was time to skip lunch. As an aside, at least the BSA had mainframe computers, and the mail-order industry at large was using metal plates that looked like dog tags, positioned in a press to imprint an address for mailing. But I digress.

Steve Jobs and Apple

Steve Jobs met his tech buddy, Steve Wozniak, at this time and joined him at the Homebrew Computer Club to demonstrate the first Apple Computer. At that time, Steve's vision was what computers could bring to people while the thrust of the computer industry was computers for major corporations. Steve Jobs's soul began to take hold at this time. He knew he was meant for something more. He was not content to just be a "geek," he wanted computers to be the "bicycle for the mind." Game on.

The people Jobs associated with were largely like Wozniak, computer code writers. Their world on computers consisted of building programs with code that gave computers instructions. There were a variety of computer languages that could be used, Jobs wanted none of this. Writing code still exists. As an example, the following is code from apple.com home page:*<link rel="alternate" href="https://www.apple.com/" hreflang="en-*

US"/><link rel="alternate" href="https://www.apple.com/ae-ar/" hreflang="ar-AE" /><link rel="alternate" href="https://www.apple. com/ae/" hreflang="en-AE" /><linkrel="alternate" href="https:// www.apple.com/am/" hreflang="en-AM" /> <link rel="alternate" href="https://www.apple.com/at/" hreflang="de-AT" /><link rel="alternate" href="https://www.apple.com/au/" hreflang="en- AU" /><link rel="alternate" href="https://www.apple.com/befr/" hreflang="fr-BE" /><link rel="alternate" href="https://www.apple. com/benl/" hreflang="nl-BE" /><linkrel="alternate" href="https:// www.apple. com/bg/" hreflang="bg-BG" /> <link rel="alternate" href="https:// w5ww.apple.com/bh-ar/" hreflang="ar-BH"/><link rel="alternate" href="https://www.apple.com/bh/" hreflang="en- BH"/><link rel="alternate" href="https://www.apple.com/br/" hreflang="pt-BR" /><link rel="alternate" href="https://www.apple.com/bw/" hreflang="en- BW" /> <link rel="alternate" href="https://www.apple. com/ca/" hreflang="en- CA" /><link rel="alternate" href="https:// www.apple.com/ca/fr/" hreflang="fr-CA" /><link rel="alternate" href="https://www.apple. com/cf/" hreflang="fr-CF" /><link rel="alternate" href="https://www.apple.com/chde/" hreflang="de-CH" /><link rel="alternate" href="https://www.apple.com/chfr/" hreflang="fr-CH" /><link rel="alternate" href="https://www.apple. com/ci/" hreflang="fr-CI" /><link rel="alternate" href="https:// www. apple.com/cl/" hreflang="es-CL" /><link rel="alternate" href="https://www.apple. com/cm/" hreflang="fr-CM" /><link rel="alternate" href="https://www.apple.com/cn/" hreflang="zh-CN" /> <link rel="alternate" href="https://www.apple.com/co/" hreflang="es-CO" /><link rel="alternate" href="https://www.apple. com/cz/" hreflang="cs-CZ" /><link

If you were operating a Microsoft operating system computer, you needed to have the ability to write code. Developers were putting together easier-to-use programs, particularly for accounting applications. But even these were designed around a user to be able to write code in order to perform many tasks.

Results are quantifiable and illustrate the acceptance of Steve Jobs as an extreme entrepreneur. I, for one, am an Apple products devotee. My first Apple computer had a monochrome screen and required the operating system to be loaded, via disc, each time the system was used. Applications and work on the Apple were stored on floppy discs, so the desktop was a sea of disc holders of all types. But being in the marketing communications business, Apple provided the freedom to create as no other computer ever had. Documents could be written and edited without white out or strike-overs. For the first time, users had a choice of typeface rather than pica and elite offered by the IBM Selectirc® typewriter. Ideas moved to electronic pages and electronic storage, editing, and printing.

Apple Products' Early Years

A coauthor and I collaborated on a 1986 business book using Apple and a desktop publishing application called *Quark Express*. By this time, the Apple had turned from a cream-colored box to a bulbus, colorful desk art that then morphed into a more computer-looking box, with a color screen. Internal operating system, applications, and electronic storage—magnificent! Over time, Apple became Macintosh and then iMac ("i" standing for internet) as the Mac was an ideal computer for World Wide Web (www) access. My agency's creative development time went from days to hours, requiring fewer people's involvement - that to me, as a business owner, meant less overhead and more flexibility.

Being in the client service business, the telephone has always been an important device. My first portable phone was mounted in my car with a box the size of a small suitcase in the trunk. Over time, this was replaced with a flip phone that could be plugged into the car or removed and used as a portable device. At one point, a telephone company client provided me with a text device that allowed me to communicate with them and a limited number of other users using the written word (text). My biggest challenge with the text device was the tiny button keyboard. Then, in 2008, the iPhone came out and quickly replaced the flip phone and its cumbersome text option and the text-only device. Communications and information access, which had been developing on the desktop, suddenly became a portable reality for voice, text, web, pictures, and video. Buttons became icons and touch screens that could scroll.

The introduction of the iPad was a true killer for printed materials, readable type, and graphics in a portable format. Wisely, Apple adopted the Kindle reader to advance books in electronic form for instant download and portable reading. After 2000, I was consulting on the use of the internet as a marketing and direct marketing tool. I was paid to speak at a conference in the newsletter industry. During a Q&A session, I was asked if the internet would replace their industry. I thought about that for a moment and said not until you can take the internet into the restroom or in front of the fireplace. And then came the iPhone, followed by the more readable iPad. Who knew, so much for printed newsletters.

From waking up until the lights are out, my iPhone and iPad are by my side, even when using my MacBook Air or Mac desktop system. On the road, my iPhone is as important as my wallet. How can I get by without my iPhone? Even if no one calls or texts, my iPhone is my lifeline to the world. I am not alone. Some additional information will support the extent to which Jobs's soul has meshed with souls around the world.

Rise of Apple Computers

Mac, since 2006, sold an estimated 116 million units (according to lifewire.com), and presently has about a 7.5 percent market share of desktop computers. The Macintosh desktop computer was introduced in 1984 with a user interface that is now copied by all types of consumer and business electronic devices that require human interactions for operation. The Mac advanced the desktop metaphor using icons for file folders, and trash cans where documents could be stored or discarded. Graphic metaphors were advanced such as colored paint brushes and pencils, and scissors that acted on screen, like their counterparts in the 3D world. There was a variety of common applications that all used the same options as user drop-downs, pop-ups, click buttons, drag-and-drop file movement, and multiple applications open at the same time. Point-and-click visual documents, cut and paste editing, and designing. No computer code is required.

They always included a mouse (or trackpad) as an interface device to expand flexibility and enhance visual activities. Using a pointer to move unrestricted around the computer and varying applications. The Mac introduced USB ports that killed multi-pin SCSI ports. Ended the floppy drive era and accelerated the CD drive's end as cloud technology advanced.

The Game-Changer iPod

Introduced in 2001, the iPod redefined the music industry. Since its launch in October 2001, until the discontinuation of its distribution, the iPod has sold 450 million units worldwide, according to Statista.com.

Reeling from online music downloads from sites like Napster. Artists were losing royalties, and music labels were losing control of distribution. Steve Jobs introduced the initial iPod to sell at $399, a price only realized a value when iTunes provided for single song music download at $.99. The availability of single-song purchases virtually killed CD sales and with it, an entire music industry staple— the record store. Today, record stores are for collectors of old vinyl records, forget setting trends through music label paid promotions. Industry-paid DJs lost control of what people listened to. Independent, non-music label artists had, for the first time, an opportunity to sell their music. And to top it all off, the sleek, no-button, metal device coupled with the Apple earbuds, became a status symbol. The control moving from the music labels to the consumer saved the recorded music industry to the benefit of the artist.

The iPod was discontinued in May 2022. With the functionality already available in iPhone, iPods have been fazed out and were now integrated to the iPhone.

iPhone and iPad: Telephones Re-Imagined

In 2020, there were about 1,042,000,000 active iPhone users (businessofapps.com) worldwide. The iPhone introduced the touch screen and retrained users in buttonless devices. It provided for sequential texting between iPhone users, which expanded to all smartphone users regardless of brand. It killed handheld, game-only devices and provided GPS for a myriad of applications. Applications to run on the iPhone could be downloaded from the online App Store and installed, just as easily as music from iTunes. Recently, there was a program on the History Channel, "100 Greatest Gadgets of All Time." After ninety-nine gadgets were examined, the number one greatest gadget of all time is the smartphone, originally introduced by IBM in 1994. It was the iPhone in 2008 that allowed the user to fully connect to the internet using a portable browser. What the iPhone put in the user's hand were:

- *Telephone*
- Answering Machine
- Video Streaming
- Music Player
- Movie Screen
- Computer
- Still Camera
- Movie Camera
- Text Messenger
- Email Messenger
- Multifunction Software Driven Device, a myriad of applications.

iPad, a tablet computer with Wi-Fi capabilities was introduced in 2010, with sales (July 2019) to be at 1.7 billion (Lifewire.com). It had a larger screen than iPhone with a font size large enough to read a book, watch a movie, portable Wi-Fi device for surfing on the couch, playing a game, taking pictures and movies, and listening to music. Take newsletters and books anywhere.

Additionally, the iPad could perform the same functions as the iPhone, above.

The Apple Watch

The Apple Watch was an unprecedented success in technology. It has created a unique breakthrough that others can only copy. The Apple Watch functions as a fitness tracker, heart rate monitor, GPS tracker, ECG readings, text messaging and so much more. According to MacRumors.com, more than one hundred million people, globally, are now own an Apple Watch.

In 2021, Apple sold more than 195 million Apple Watches since Series 0, according to headphonesaddict.com. The market share of Apple Watches is increasing year after year. As an example, in Quarter 4 of 2020, it held around 48% smartwatch market share. In 2021, it has grown to 51.4%, according to Gitnux Blog.

Apple Services

Apple services allow you to subscribe to services exclusive for apple users: iCloud, Apple Music, Apple TV+, Apple Arcade, Apple News+, Apple Fitness+ in 2020: 620,000,000 (businessofapps. com)

There are other products such as AirPods, and by the time this book is released, there will probably be more products. But you get the message. The soul of Steve Jobs permeates all of Apple products and attracts the souls of faithful Apple users worldwide. Putting technology of many types in the hands of ordinary people has and will continue to change the world. It allowed connectivity to become easy and hand-held. He created a shortcut for everything that others felt was too impossible.

Jobs and the "Dent in the Universe"

Steve Jobs, without a doubt, left a dent in the universe. Through these amazing technological advancements that he launched with his partners, the world was never the same again. He revolutionized the way cellular phones work, and brought entrepreneurship to the next level - he brought forth something that will be more pleasing to people than that which currently exists.

He was a perfect example of an entrepreneur – someone who anchored his motivations not on money but of the soul's mission to put a dent in the universe. He was passionate, resourceful, creative, process-oriented, and disciplined. He had the traits of a successful entrepreneur. Without Steve Jobs, however, other entrepreneurs in this world might still come up and discover other technological advancements that could shape the world. But Jobs came up with an advancement that is uniquely his.

Samsung, Huawei, and other cellphone manufacturers may come up with similar technology, but Jobs made sure that his idea was a pioneer – his entrepreneurial idea came first above all else. This is how he made a dent in the universe.

Becoming an outstanding entrepreneur in this competitive world, therefore, means being the first one to discover an advancement that could bring change to your customers, and most importantly, a benchmark for others to follow.

Chapter 10

Jesus Christ

From 12 disciples to 2.2 billion believers in a span of two thousand years. Without a doubt, Jesus's life and teachings go beyond mere history. The magnitude of his life goes far beyond any man who walked on this planet. His beginnings were humble, His death was tragic, and His teachings were timeless. The Bible is the bestselling book of all time, with 5 billion copies distributed to date, and translated into 3,350 languages. It is the most widely-translated book of all time. Ever.

Looking at these astounding figures, one would come into thinking: What was Jesus's element that brought his endeavor to success?

Let's start where it all began. Jesus was born to a teenager. He was taken out of the country for his own safety. Returning several years later to Nazareth where he learned to be a carpenter like his father while spending as much time as possible in the temple, learning from and questioning the synagogue leaders. The Jewish synagogue of that day was very structured, based on the rules delivered in The Torah, which consists of Genesis, Exodus, Leviticus, Numbers, Deuteronomy, and Joshua, for how God's people were to get along. Prior to Exodus, the Israelites were slaves, following the rules of their Egyptian "owners," so a new set of rules was necessary for the people to survive as a free culture.

The keeping of societal and theological rules fell to the landless Levites who, over time, formalized their role as keepers of all life rules. There were rules governing all facets of daily life. Rules, if not followed, would bring scorn and disfavor from God, according to the Levites. So Jews lived in constant fear, doled out by their synagogue. But this was not their only fear, the Roman occupiers of the Jewish land were also feared. So the Jewish people had little hope. It was far easier to, "go along to get along." Independent, free will was subordinated as a way to get by.

Jesus's life is unaccounted for from age twelve to age thirty when He began his ministry. Getting underway at age thirty, Jesus began putting together his disciples, whom he planned on mentoring to share his explanation of God with all peoples. To make a statement, He turned water into wine so a wedding feast could continue, considered His first miracle. Much of Jesus's teaching used parables, which are short stories that teach a moral or spiritual lesson. One example is the parable of the two sons. One son asked for his inheritance and left to lose everything. When he came back, the father threw a feast welcoming him back, illustrating forgiveness on this earth, an act of love. He explained the love God has for all of us and His boundless forgiveness. There are thirty-one unique parables in the Gospels, each one intended to be revisited as they have been for two thousand years.

He also demanded attention when he overturned the table of the money changers, which were part of the worship service facilitators. Jesus was a rebel. His intentions were to not only upset the moneychanger tables but to upset the entire apple cart of the day (no pun intended as it pertains to Apple computers). For Jesus, the main thing was to teach love for oneself and others, which was counter to the teachings of the synagogue leaders.

The Turning Point

One day, the Pharisees asked the adult Jesus, "When will the kingdom of God begin?"

Jesus replied, "The kingdom of God isn't ushered in with visible signs. You won't be able to say, 'It has begun here in this place or there in that part of the country.' For the kingdom of God is within you" (Luke 17:20–21 TLB).

This was a revolutionary comment and became the turning point of how the world will be governed thereafter. God was no longer out there somewhere to be interpreted by the Pharisees; God is within each one of us. And since this is the case, each of us has the innate capability of realizing the word of God, as delivered by Jesus's teachings. Jesus did not care if one was Jewish or Gentile, all people had God within. No one was chosen over anyone else.

Jesus taught, "Ask, and it shall be given to you; seek, and you shall find; knock, and it and to him who knocks it shall be opened" (Matthew 7:7–8 NAS). These were big ideas for the oppressed peoples who heard Jesus, both Jews, and Gentiles. God was drawn closer to the people. Jesus gave a fresh idea of a God: a God who can be tapped anytime – a more personal connection.

Adding to this, He gave people hope, that there is a way to improve life. He went on to say, "Come to me, all who are weary and heavy-laden, and I will give you rest. Take my yoke upon you, and learn from me, for I am gentle and humble in heart; and you shall find rest."

A person's soul would be put to rest if that person followed Jesus's teachings. Makes the soul connection, which is as true today as it was, almost two thousand years ago.

Soul, Love, God

We previously discussed Jesus's teaching, "love your neighbor as yourself," one of the foundational teachings that must have and do resonate with many souls. Today, there are approximately 2.1 billion Christians globally (religiouspopulation.com) with the largest concentrations in Western Europe, North America, and South America. This represents approximately 28 percent of the world's population. Quite a following from one person's teachings in a time when there were no mass communications, no internet, few books, and intentional suppression of any authority except that of Rome. Jesus's message of love, as the means to a satisfied soul, was meant to and has resonated with many people.

Jesus brought forth a winning combination. He brought together three variables: soul, love, and God. This provided a vastly new concept for each human. We each have God within us, so we have the ability to understand what God would have us know. We each have a soul that influences and often impels us to take action. And the actions we take are to be based on love, being loved, and loving others, all others.

In John 13:34, Jesus clearly defined it: "A new commandment I give to you, that you love one another: Just as I have loved you, you also are to love one another." Love was his foundation of teaching – in this verse, he defined the kind of love we ought to share and that is the same magnitude of love He has for us.

Jesus' Teachings as Foundation of Laws

It took about 1,800 years for Jesus's teachings about love and *God within* to be adopted by a governing body – a government created by minds from the thirteen colonies that became to be known as the United States. Several kindred souls bonded to create the oppressed colonies' position statement that would end England's rule, the Declaration of Independence. The opening statement set forth a unified set of beliefs as the strategy to create a new government:

"We hold these truths to be self-evident, that all men are created equal, that they are endowed by their Creator with certain unalienable Rights, that among these are Life, Liberty and the pursuit of Happiness."

This was a recognition of Jesus's teaching that God within us gives us unalienable rights. In other words, the right to life liberty, and the pursuit of happiness are not granted by the government but by God to every individual; thus, negating the authority of governments over the governed. But to make sure that the US government would never have the ability to subdue the governed,

70

this body of minds in the late 1700s put together the governing rule book, the US Constitution. The preamble reads:

We the People of the United States, in Order to form a more perfect Union, establish Justice, insure domestic Tranquility, provide for the common defense, promote the general Welfare, and secure the Blessings of Liberty to ourselves and our Posterity, do ordain and establish this Constitution for the United States of America.

The constitution then goes into the branches of government and the expectations of each branch. But the most important to the individual became known as the Bill of Rights, that are contained in the first ten amendments. The following are those amendments that, if read in the context of protecting the individual, illustrate the genius of the authors of the document. Read the following in the context of a person living in Jesus's time to gain a perspective of how Jesus's teachings were manifest in these writings. These individual rights, framed in the love for the individual, define what the government cannot do in order to protect the individual from oppression, thus ending the fear of government.

First Amendment. Congress shall make no law respecting an establishment of religion, or prohibiting the free exercise thereof, or abridging the freedom of speech, or of the press; or the right of the people peaceably to assemble, and to petition the Government for a redress of grievances.

Second Amendment. A well-regulated Militia, being necessary to the security of a free State, the right of the people to keep and bear Arms, shall not be infringed.

Third Amendment. No Soldier shall, in time of peace be quartered in any house, without the consent of the Owner, nor in time of war, but in a manner to be prescribed by law.

Fourth Amendment. The right of the people to be secure in their persons, houses, papers, and effects, against unreasonable searches and seizures, shall not be violated, and no Warrants shall issue, but upon probable cause, supported by Oath or affirmation, and particularly describing the place to be searched, and the persons or things to be seized.

Fifth Amendment. No person shall be held to answer for a capital, or otherwise infamous crime, unless on a presentment or indictment of a Grand Jury, except in cases arising in the land or naval forces, or in the Militia, when in actual service in time of War or public danger; nor shall any person be subject for the same offense to be twice put in jeopardy of life or limb; nor shall be compelled in any criminal case to be a witness against himself, nor be deprived of life, liberty, or property, without due process of law; nor shall private property be taken for public use, without just compensation.

Sixth Amendment. In all criminal prosecutions, the accused shall enjoy the right to a speedy and public trial, by an impartial jury of the State and district wherein the crime shall have been committed, which district shall have been previously ascertained by law, and to be informed of the nature and cause of the accusation; to be confronted with the witnesses against him; to have compulsory process for obtaining witnesses in his favor, and to have the Assistance of Counsel for his defense.

Seventh Amendment. In Suits at common law, where the value in controversy shall exceed twenty dollars, the right of trial by jury shall be preserved, and no fact tried by a jury shall be otherwise re-examined in any Court of the United States than according to the rules of the common law.

Eighth Amendment. Excessive bail shall not be required, nor excessive fines imposed, nor cruel and unusual punishments inflicted.

Ninth Amendment. The enumeration in the Constitution, of certain rights, shall not be construed to deny or disparage others retained by the people.

Tenth Amendment. The powers not delegated to the United States by the Constitution, nor prohibited by it to the States, are reserved to the States respectively, or to the people.

The rebel, Jesus Christ, started a revolution among humans that took almost eighteen hundred years to become the foundation for governing the people of the United States. His influence is global, but the only governing body that is based on his person-centric teachings is the United States. Today, there are estimated to be about 70 percent of the US population that has some soul connection to Jesus Christ, by identifying as Christians.

Jesus, the individual, lived as he taught. Jesus, the messenger of God, put the individual in the center of life and ask that each person to, "love your neighbor as yourself."

Jesus and the Mission

Jesus had a mission of turning fear to love. It was not a very easy job to do and He knew about it. He had to hurdle the challenges and bear the pains accompanied by the spread of his unconventional teachings. He had to face rejection, doubts, and persecution, leading to his ultimate death. He knew very well that spreading his message would mean upsetting church leaders and the society so established by the laws of fear. He knew that his message would result in him facing a deadly ending, but he trod forward. He ate with the sinners and tax collectors – which brought fury from His critics who campaigned against him.

But Jesus ultimately held the qualities of an entrepreneur that we studied in the previous chapters – He was a risk-taker, He was self-aware, disciplined, and self-motivated. To bring his message of love to the world, he knew where to start.

Disciplined to achieve the goal, he picked 12 imperfect disciples – uneducated commoners at that – to be with him on a mission. If the mission was to run a business, this would be a bad business idea. From a marketing perspective, choosing disciples who were imperfect commoners is sure to bring a negative business impact. But this was the message he wants to bring out – that in a society where only the powerful have control, God can choose the common people if they only believe.

This message now leveled the playing field for everyone and to the generations succeeding it: that those common people can obtain God's righteousness, and no matter the weight of your sin, forgiveness is free if you repent and believe.

Chapter 11

So What?

We have discussed two individuals and their accomplishments, in the context of how they were successful in transmitting their souls to the world. Both have changed the world forever. One harnessed technology for use by all humans. One turned life from fear to love. One has millions of product users worldwide. One has over two billion followers worldwide. But both individuals have souls that have not yet been bought into their souls.

Let's face it. There are people who dislike Apple products for a variety of reasons. However, the technology products they choose often have Apple-like, ease-of-use interfaces. Apple sued Microsoft for many years for "knocking off" the graphical user interface (GUI) that Apple developed. So while Apple may not be the brand of choice, makers of "me too" Apple products are taking advantage of Steve Jobs's soul by engineering their products to simulate Apple products. And Apple has done its fair share of using other product concepts to develop its own products. For example, the first wrist-mounted communications device was introduced by Dick Tracy in a 1946 comic strip about a crime fighter who used such a device. Today, the Apple Watch is a multi-function device far exceeding Dick Tracy's single-function device.

Apple computer is now the most valuable brand in the world, still leveraging the soul of Steve Jobs in an ever-advancing array of products that effortlessly deliver technologies for use by humans. Products that continue to provide the "bicycle for the mind" as Jobs envisioned. The backbone Apple product, the iPhone, is faster and more capable now than it was in 2007, but it is still the same product. The big idea has been improved upon, but there is no new big idea. This is true for all Apple products developed under the supervision of Steve Jobs. Today's products have added features – two of the most significant features are their speed of function and camera – but do, basically, what they have always done.

This is not a criticism of Apple management. It is, rather, the result of an extreme entrepreneur, a person who truly has "put a dent in the universe." Steve Jobs's soul went into Apple products, and his soul continues to attract and keep Apple product users. As hard as they try, Apple will always be dependent on Steve Jobs's soul for their success. Not until there is a technological paradigm shift, like the one Jobs introduced, will Apple products fall out of favor. I (we), the user(s), share the experience Steve Jobs wanted us to have, and we continue to do so. In truth, the one thing that Apple management can do is walk away from Steve Jobs' soul and take Apple in another direction. This would be the end of Apple Computer.

As far as sharing the soul of Jesus Christ, it is not binary, *love or fear*. It seems humanly impossible to you to express a soul governed only by love or to express a soul governed only by fear. We all live in a dynamic world where we have degrees of love and degrees of fear. This continuum also has levels of emotion from *indifference to passionate*. The graphic in Figure 1 provides a visual of these concepts juxtaposed, creating a four-square matrix that will serve as the basis for the discussion about exercising, or not, the change that Jesus brings us.

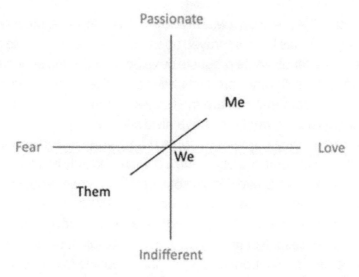

Figure 1

The X-axis provides the change that Jesus brought to humans, the movement from fear as the state of being to one of love. The Y axis expands the fear and love continuum, to include the emotional aspects of or intensity from a level of *indifferent to passionate*. This axis is where our souls really influence our decisions by controlling our emotions.

To look at the four quadrants separately, *Quadrants 1,* passionate and fear is the world Jesus addressed. The world of fear of the church and fear of the Roman occupiers. Passionate intensity means fear is engendered in order to control the population. The intensity comes from the governing and not the governed. The individual is virtually powerless in this quadrant. In today's terms, the same fears of government exist in any society that sets freedom-restricting rules for the people. Rules that, if not followed, have negative consequences. In Quadrant 1, the negative consequences could be death, incarceration, loss of property, public shaming, and/or fines.

Quadrant 3, fear and indifference, are rules that the imposing authority is less concerned with enforcing. An example is a crosswalk. A person who does not use the government-defined pathway across a street crossing in mid-block is j-walking. The government's attempt to control where to cross the street was even marked, but a seldom enforced rule. Consequences for j-walking can be a fine, public service time, or public shaming.

Quadrant 2, passionate and love, would be where Jesus would have been and taught that is where we all should be. "Love your neighbor as yourself." In today's culture, this quadrant would include churches and charitable organizations dedicated to serving and/or helping people. There is no force to perform in this quadrant. It is up to the individual to participate. The reward is a contented soul doing what one is free to do. So many people seek out opportunities to "do good" for others.

Quadrant 4, indifferent and love, is the vast majority of the population. People who have lives and occupations are not in the charitable realm. Making a living and doing or giving a little from time to time to help others. People in this quadrant are generally pleasant to others they come in contact with. They are free to help others or not without concern.

The big divide in Figure 1 is the left side and the right side. The left side contains forces that want to control the individual's freedoms. The right side allows freedom of choice as to how to "love thy neighbor." Expressions of this can take many forms. None of them were compelled by others but rather driven from within.

Figure 1 provides us with the characteristics of fear and love expanded by passion, or not; however, this explanation does not illustrate the dynamic life. There is the action dimension, the Z axis (See Figure 2) the *them, we,* and *me* axis. This is the action axis. What is being done or projected to whom and by whom as actors delivering the approach, and there are those receiving what is being delivered. The action axis has three actors or recipients—*them, we, and me. Them* is any group of people that does not include you (which can be extrapolated to be a single person). *We* is any group that does include you. *Me* is if you are the only participant in a group.

Any group can take actions that engender fear or love, passionately or indifferently. By the same token, any group can be acted upon by fear or love, passionately or indifferently. This brings us full circle to the chapter on the soul. In that chapter were concentric circles of relationships based on the attraction of our souls. These soul attractions that are positive create the *we* groups. Soul attractions that are not positive create the *them* groups. But one group we all participate in is the *me* group.

The interesting dimension of the action axis is that each of us fluctuates from being a sender to being a receiver on a moment-to-moment basis.

Life Interpretations, Applications

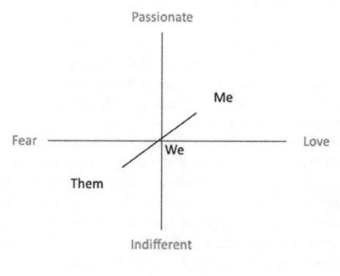

Figure 2

An example of how to apply these concepts is to look at the government. Presently, I am an elected state representative. As a legislator, my legislative existence is to make/edit/change state laws. Every year, the state legislature considers five hundred to seven hundred bills that may or may not go into law. All of the state legislation fit in Figure 2. A bill is either going to restrict personal liberty by using a penalty (fear) or allow an activity that has previously not been permitted (love).

My emotional involvement in any bill determines my interest and commitment to support and even work for a bill. In my first term, there was a passionate one-hour debate about lead sinkers used for weighing down a fishing line. The bill was to ban the sale and use of lead sinkers in the state. The bill's sponsors and supporters gave passionate speeches about how lead sinkers might kill loons, a migratory aquatic bird - when the bird ingests it. Opponents of the bill indicated that there is no such record of any such ingested sinker loon deaths.

I haven't been fishing since my childhood, so my interest in lead sinkers was certainly indifferent. Representations that there are no sinker-ingested loon deaths mitigated my interest in the topic, also to a level of indifference. However, since there were alternatives to lead sinkers and loon populations are down in the state, maybe a supportive vote banning lead sinkers could be better (love) than not supporting the bill. I don't remember how I voted, but the bill passed and lead sinkers were to be phased out of use in the state.

The lead sinker is not the point of this example. The point is that we are all presented with situations about which we have no knowledge or emotional investment. Most of the time through presentations, news, social media, or however the situation is presented, we are not inclined or forced to make a decision for or against it. So we let most situations pass. In day-to-day living, we don't have to have a position in every situation. What is interesting about the lead sinker vote is that the vote did favor the love of loons that might ingest a lead sinker and die over the traditional lead sinker.

The legislature (we) passed a law that affects those that fish (them). Inasmuch as those who fish are not politically organized, I doubt we will hear much about this piece of legislation. Nor will bird watchers (them) make a big noise about this legislation. In both cases, however, from their perspective, the legislature is *them,* and the fishing community and bird watchers are both *we.* From a legislative standpoint, we passed a law that phased out lead sinkers, and I'm sure there is some type of fine for failure to do so. In our way, we put fear into action in order to accomplish the desired outcome, no more lead sinkers or dead loons from ingesting them.

Our society seems to be made up of a never-ending supply of *we* versus *them.* We can set up all kinds of groups based on sex, race, gender, national origin, eye color, weight, political affiliation, wealth, education, height, vehicle preference, age, religious preference, favored writing hand, athletic abilities, sports team favorites, news channel preference, media preference, sexual attitudes, memberships, veteran status, employers, social affiliations, elected status, influence, authority, profession, and plus whatever I have left out. There will be no exhaustive debate on these pages about all of the options and permutations that can occur, especially as each one of us can identify with more than one group while continuing to be an individual.

Our identities are in our souls, and the intensity of any group relationship is our personal struggle or acquiescence within ourselves. The *me* can be in conflict within even when the relationship is *we*. It is in our nature to not always agree with the positions of one or more of our *we* affiliations.

Reflections from the Lives of the Extreme Entrepreneurs

So where are *we,* if the extreme entrepreneurs are *them?* At this point, many of us know we will never be extreme entrepreneurs, but like *them,* we can follow the convictions of our souls to fulfilling that which we have within us, placed there by the manufacturer. Perhaps, we will never "change the world," but we can change our world! We can let go of our current vine and seek another, hoisted by our confidence in our main thing.

What in our world do we think needs to be different? Are we looking at incremental changes or entire paradigm shifts? Are changes needed to things or people? Which changes are going to have the most profound effects? Changes to *them, we* or *me?* Clearly, the only control we have is over the *me,* so that's probably where we should start.

Write down your parables, your habitual actions, and decide if they are based on fear or in love. Is your motivation to earn money out of fear of starving and being homeless, or is it done in love to provide for yourself and your loved ones? I would suggest that if your efforts are out of fear, you probably don't like your job. However, if your efforts are out of love, you enjoy your job.

You can repeat this exercise for all facets of your life. Your relationships. Your appearance. Your favorite music. In each area, are your decisions motivated by fear of being excluded or love of being included?

Remember: *The outcome of fear is never love. The outcome of love is never fear.*

When we start to change our perspective and begin to do things from the heart, it changes everything. We become more passionate, driven, and motivated with joy that flows from within. While our physical bodies have their limitations, when we start doing things out of love, we don't feel the physical drain that it causes no matter how tedious.

Let us look into our souls and listen to what it tells us. When we start doing so, our compass – our soul – will take us in the right direction where we ought to be. I believe that each of our souls is meant for something greater than ourselves.

Search for it within you. Find it.

Bibliography

Bible, NIV.

Fernandez, Ivan. *Think Like Steve Jobs,* 2018.

Isaacson, Walter. *Steve Jobs.* Simon & Schuster, 2011, 2013.

Kerns, Tom, Dr. Plato's Republic and Phaedrus. North Seattle Community College, Philosophy 101 Online Course, The Three Parts of the Soul.

MacArthur, John. *Twelve Ordinary Men.* Thomas Nelson, 2002.

McLuhan, Marshall. *Understanding Media: The Extensions of Man.* Mentor New York, 1964, republished 1994 MIT Press.

Ortberg, John. *Soul Keeping.* Zondervan, 2014.

Quizlet.com—an educational site with over three hundred million user generated flashcard sets and over fifty million users. Contributor could not be found.

Rohr, Richard. *Falling Upward.* Jossey-Bass, A Wiley Imprint, 2011.

Rohr, Richard. *Soul of All Things.* Center for Action and Contemplation, March 5, 2018, online.

Rohr, Richard, *The Universal Christ. Center* for Action and Contemplation, Inc., Published by Convergent Books, 2019.

The Gospel of Thomas. Original translation by the Berlin Working Group for Coptic Gnostic Writings. Taken from Synopsis Quattuor Evangelorium, 2nd corrected printing, 1997. As modified by Stephen J. Patterson and James M. Robinson in Patterson, Robinson, and Bethge. The Fifth Gospel, Trinity Press International, 1998.

The Reverend Deborah Knowlton, Advisor.

Zhi Gang Sha, Dr. The Power of Soul. Atria Books, a division of Simon &Schuster, Inc., 2009.

About the Author

The author is a very busy retired individual. He has authored two marketing books, operated a direct marketing agency for twenty years, and spent ten years in marketing and business development consulting. While writing this work, he served as a state representative, moderator of his church, and chair of his town's planning board. He has taught at several universities at the graduate level. He has been married to his wife for fifty-three years, has two children and five grandchildren. His education includes a BA in philosophy, a master's in business administration (MBA), and a PhD in business administration.

Printed in the USA
CPSIA information can be obtained
at www.ICGtesting.com
LVHW051152220324
775202LV00003B/621